Praise f

MW01006101

Our culture sends two strong messages about work: either that it only holds value for personal gain, or that it is not worth the effort at all. *Called to Cultivate* deftly uses Scripture to remind us that the believer's work is divinely infused with redemptive kingdom potential. Chelsea Sobolik points to the blessing of work as worship, and its purpose for the flourishing of our families, friends, churches, and communities. Whether you serve in the marketplace, church, home, or all three, take up and find new hope when that early-morning alarm signals the start of a new day.

K. A. ELLIS

Director of the Edmiston Center at Reformed Theological Seminary in Atlanta

Chelsea Sobolik is a seasoned professional and a faithful believer whose insights and experiences in the work world will help prepare and guide those starting out as well as those already facing challenges and questions in their working lives. This book is a gift to those who want to work well, serve well, and live well.

KAREN SWALLOW PRIOR

Author of *On Reading Well: Finding the Good Life Through Great Books*

In *Called to Cultivate*, Chelsea zooms in on some of the most relatable (yet rarely well-articulated) issues that Christian women face navigating the world of work. In the warm voice of a friend, she guides the reader with practical wisdom and advice for navigating the personal, physical, and spiritual aspects of our lives as working women. This was the book I didn't even realize I needed!

ERICKA ANDERSEN

Author of *Reason to Return: Why Women Need the Church and the Church Needs Women*

With refreshing authenticity and candor, Chelsea addresses key questions facing today's Christian women navigating the unique dynamics of professional development, life balance, and effective advocacy. This book offers a grace-filled invitation to readers to better understand their God-given purpose and confidently leverage their influence with an eternal perspective.

RUTH MALHOTRA

Writer, speaker, and Manager of Strategic Partnerships at Ronald Blue Trust

CALLED TO CULTIVATE

A GOSPEL VISION FOR WOMEN AND WORK

CHELSEA PATTERSON SOBOLIK

MOODY PUBLISHERS
CHICAGO

All emphasis in Scripture has been added.

A version of the section "Created as Ezers" first appeared in the author's book *Longing for Motherhood: Holding On to Hope in the Midst of Childlessness* (Chicago: Moody Publishers, 2018).

Names and details of some stories have been changed to protect the privacy of individuals.

Published in association with The Bindery Agency, www.TheBinderyAgency.com.

Edited by Amanda Cleary Eastep
Interior design: Ragont Design
Cover design: Faceout Studio, Spencer Fuller

Author photo: robertmatthewsphoto.com

ISBN: 978–0-8024–2807–3

Originally delivered by fleets of horse-drawn wagons, the affordable paperbacks from D. L. Moody's publishing house resourced the church and served everyday people. Now, after more than 125 years of publishing and ministry, Moody Publishers' mission remains the same—even if our delivery systems have changed a bit. For more information on other books (and resources) created from a biblical perspective, go to www.moodypublishers.com or write to:

Moody Publishers
820 N. LaSalle Boulevard
Chicago, IL 60610

1 3 5 7 9 10 8 6 4 2

Printed in the United States of America

For my mom, Christie, and my mother-in-law, Liz—thank you both for modeling what it means to work well, to create, to tend to the hearts of children, and to glorify the Lord in everything you do. How richly blessed I am by you both.

For all the women who work—may you always remember how much your work matters in the kingdom of God.

Contents

Introduction

I was barely three months into my new marriage when I abruptly lost my job. Stunned and hurt, I began picking up the pieces of my professional life and patching it back together. At the time, I was working on Capitol Hill, and the member of Congress I was working for resigned in the middle of his term, resulting in the entire staff losing their jobs. While our paychecks didn't cease immediately, the pressure was on to find a new job. As I began a demoralizing job search, I was still reeling from the shock of the unexpected loss.

At the same time, I was stepping into my new role as a wife and learning the new rhythms of married life. Additionally, I was a few months shy of releasing my first book, *Longing for Motherhood*, into the world. It felt as if every area of my life was changing all at once. The work I'd done on Capitol Hill was thrilling, and I eagerly looked forward to going into work each morning, where I sought favorable public policy solutions. Many of the policies I worked on were focused on alleviating the pain and suffering of vulnerable people, and I found deep fulfillment in my work. This wasn't just a job loss for me. In many ways, it was a loss of identity. I had been working my dream job, until it suddenly came crashing down around me.

By God's kindness, I quickly found a job as an executive assistant, but I didn't enjoy the work. My days were filled with scheduling meetings and filing expense reports. A colleague at the firm was occasionally unkind in their communication toward me, and I'd slip off to the bathroom to cry over their hurtful words. The posture of my heart was more inclined toward grumbling than gratitude for the Lord's provision. But I was determined to serve with excellence, even on the difficult days. When I left, my boss told me that I was the best executive assistant he'd ever had.

In the midst of that challenging job, I began to wrestle with the topic of work. Did my feelings of frustration and angst matter to God? Was it okay for me to desire more from my work? Or was striving for excellence in my role enough?

Growing up, I'd set my heart on moving overseas to become a missionary and work with vulnerable children. My parents lived in West Africa before they started a family, and I hung on every word when they shared stories of their time in Togo. I'm adopted from Eastern Europe and have a deep burden for children in need of safety and permanency. In college, I studied international relations and French to prepare myself for a move to West Africa. After graduating, I moved home long enough to fill out an application for a mission's program. As I was applying, I sensed the Lord asking me to stop the process.

Excuse me, Lord? Did I hear You correctly?
You want me to stop pursuing this dream I've had for years?

As I prayed, the answer became clear—the Lord was redirecting my steps. Even though I was confused, I obediently stepped away from the application process. Instead of getting ready to pack my bags and catch a one-way international flight, I felt stuck at home with no direction about what to do next.

During college, I had served as the senior class president, and after graduation, was asked to speak at a conference in Washington,

DC. There, I ran into a friend who suggested I interview for a job opening at the nonprofit where she worked. Having nothing to lose, I interviewed and was offered the job. I prayed about it, sensed the Lord directing my steps to DC, packed my bags, and moved. While my time in DC has held many difficult moments, it's also been filled with sweet gifts. I've made dear friends, I met and married my husband, and I've planted deep roots. I've chosen to stay, invest in my community, and give back more than I take.

Over the years, my understanding of and relationship with work has deepened. Truthfully, before my job loss, I hadn't spent much time examining the topic of work in light of Scripture. While I've had some professional mentors, those relationships didn't go beyond beefing up my professional skills. I didn't have many examples of how to connect a theology of work to the practical day-to-day issues and questions I wrestled with as a Christian woman in the workplace. All of us bring different stories, experiences, and desires to this topic.

Perhaps your professional life has had plenty of ups and downs. Perhaps you're struggling to find contentment and purpose in your current role. Perhaps you're unemployed and would be elated to find a job. Perhaps you're pursuing a side hustle while working full time or caring for children and managing a household. Perhaps you never intended to be a working mom, but financial strain in your family propelled you into the workforce. Perhaps you're navigating a new working situation because of the impact of the COVID-19 pandemic. No two situations are alike, but there are biblical principles and helpful rhythms we can put into place so we can flourish holistically.

The reality is, work goes well beyond what we do for a paycheck. All of us work in many different capacities—caring for the needs of others (children, aging parents, or neighbors), serving at church, volunteering in the community, managing our finances and households, and maintaining orderly lives. All these activities are work and therefore matter deeply.

The Bible is far from silent on the topic of work. In the first pages of Scripture, we see God at work, creating and cultivating. He skillfully and beautifully created the sun, moon, and stars, land and sky, plants and animals; and in the culmination of creation, He designed man and woman after His own image. After He created Adam and Eve, He called them to work—to fill the earth and subdue it, have dominion over every living thing, tend the garden, name the animals, and actively participate in cultivation. God designed work to be good for us, and He invites us to image Him by working.

Most of our waking hours are filled with working in some capacity, and we ought to devote serious thought and consideration to what the Bible says about it. How do we honor the Lord in and through our work? How can we, as Christian women, navigate working? And what are the best practices and rhythms that will allow us to thrive?

Our situations will differ. Some of us have bosses. Some of us are self-employed. Some of us are tempted toward people pleasing. Some of us are tempted toward laziness. Some of us cringe when we hear the alarm clock go off in the morning because we're exhausted, and we must get up and do it all again. Some of us are struggling to make ends meet and are living paycheck to paycheck. Some of us are trying to care for our children, while working the hours expected of us.

Wherever you find yourself, I want to remind you that the Lord sees you and loves you. It might feel like you're working in obscurity or that your work doesn't matter. But as God's child, you are never alone in your work. The Lord has promised never to leave or forsake you, no matter how challenging and overwhelming life feels. As I was wrestling through my job loss and figuring out my next steps, this truth of God's enduring presence gave me deep comfort. I was reminded that no matter what my professional life looked like, no matter how many accomplishments or failures I had, God was guiding my path.

And He's leading yours too.

My hope is that this book equips you to think carefully about how and why you work, how to tackle challenges and opportunities, how to lead well, and how to build a flourishing life. May we stop dreading Monday and rushing toward Friday, and instead faithfully invest ourselves in the work the Lord has called us to do.

Chapter 1

Designed to Work

How We Reflect God's Nature When We Work

Work of all kinds, whether with the hands or the mind, evidences our dignity as human beings—because it reflects the image of God the Creator in us.

Tim Keller[1]

Since the beginning of time, humanity has been a working people, and women have played a vital role in the flourishing of the church, their communities, and the kingdom of God through their work. Without the work of women, the world would look radically different. Women have fiercely defended the most vulnerable, built businesses that creatively solve problems, and served others with their giftings, skills, and passions. Women play a vital role in God's call to work, to create, and to advance His kingdom. We were created to work, but it can look different for each one of us. We tend to have a range of reactions to work, and our relationship with it can be a mixed bag, especially depending on our season of life.

Underpaid and overworked.
Exhausted and overwhelmed.
Passionate and driven.
Purposeless and frustrated.
Excited and energized.

For some of us, our hearts are lit on fire when we work because we feel like we're making a difference in the lives of others, or we're passionately pursuing a dream. Others of us experience frustration, discouragement, and disappointment. For most of us, we're somewhere in between. We have good days when we're energized, productive, and connecting our work to God's mission. We hit our goals or complete the project ahead of schedule. Or maybe we receive a promotion. We likely all have difficult days that fill us with frustration, weariness, and dissatisfaction. Our coworkers get on our nerves, our boss hasn't communicated clearly, and we fall further and further behind on emails. Additionally, while work is deeply meaningful, it shouldn't be ultimate in our lives. We were created to work, but we were also created for rest, play, and pleasure.

This book was born out of my desire to explore certain concepts and answer certain questions. I found plenty of books on a biblical approach to work and vocation, but not as many specifically helping Christian women think through this topic. Women face unique opportunities and challenges within work, and I've personally wrestled through many of them myself. Women wrestle with questions like:

Is it wrong for me to pursue my career ambitions?

If I step back for a season to raise children, will I be able to enter back into the workforce?

How do I glorify the Lord with my work?

How do I balance work and life?

How do I deal with a bad boss and respectfully stand up for myself at work?

Should I pursue higher education if I'm going to get married and have children soon?

Should I work outside the home if I have young children?

Chances are, if you're reading this book, you're one of those women trying to navigate these and other questions. The majority of people spend approximately 90,000 hours of their lives working.[2] Yet many of us don't consider why we work, where we work, or even how we approach our work. I want you to be equipped to step into a meaningful vocation, know how to lead well, navigate challenges, and press into opportunities. Fundamental to all of that is grasping a deep understanding of *why* you work. Because the *why* changes everything.

But to really understand work, we must go back . . .

Back to a garden . . .

A BIBLICAL CALL TO WORK

The opening pages of Scripture show God skillfully creating the earth and the heavens, sun and stars, birds and beasts. His words created worlds. After each day of creation, He declared His work to be good.[3] The first chapters of Genesis begin to tell us about who God is and what He cares about. God's original design for the world is clearly communicated in how and why He ordered the world. Creation contains order, beauty, excellence, and ultimately points us to the glory of God.

Created in God's Image

The pinnacle of creation is humanity. God created us in His very own image, and we are distinct from every other created thing. Bearing the image of the Almighty means every single person has dignity and worth. We are inherently valuable to God. Our dignity as people isn't dependent upon our *ability*, or based upon what we *do*, but rather, in who we *are*. Theologian Russell Moore says that "humans are created to picture God and God's care for, God's love of, and God's rule over the rest of creation."[4] The purpose of being made in God's image is to tell the world about who God is.

God created two distinct sexes—male and female—in His image and gave them both dominion over the earth. Author Kathy Keller reminds us that "we are called to be a reflection of the image of God, in our gendered humanity."[5] Our sex isn't an accident. It is a part of God's good design for humanity and one of the ways we display to the world what He is like. Being created female, says Keller, comes with "gifts and responsibilities" that we must steward "if we are to truly reflect the accurate image of God."[6]

Far too many women, myself included, have experienced sexism, both in society and in the workplace. We'll explore this in depth in later chapters, but it's important to acknowledge that women throughout history have been mistreated simply because they are female. Gender-based mistreatment is antithetical to how God created and ordered the world, and we ought to push back whenever women aren't treated with the dignity, worth, and value they inherently possess. A woman's worth and her work should be honored because God declared His creation and His calling for men and women to be very good.[7]

As we grasp the beauty of bearing God's image, it inevitably reshapes how we view and treat other humans. This is what motivates Christians to be on the forefront of fighting against injustices around the world—protecting the preborn, caring for vulnerable children and families, alleviating poverty and food insecurity, and fighting for more just institutions and systems. It's why Christians ought to be the ones most robustly proclaiming God's care and design for every single person, especially those that society tries to devalue—the weak, the vulnerable, the elderly, those with disabilities, and those who look different from us.

A proper understanding of the *imago Dei* helps us discern our purpose, worth, identity, limitations, stewardship responsibilities, and how we interact with other image bearers. Scripture reorients us toward a holistic vision of humanity. Humans matter because God created us in His image, and that changes everything.

Creation Mandate

Work predates the fall. God blessed Adam and Eve and gave them the creation mandate, which is the "on-going charge to humanity, in the power and blessing of God, to be fruitful, multiply, and fill the earth and to gently subdue and cultivate the earth."[8] In Genesis, we see that both men *and* women are commanded to subdue and exercise dominion over the earth.

> And God blessed *them*. And God said to *them*, "Be fruitful and multiply and fill the earth and subdue it, and have dominion over the fish of the sea and over the birds of the heavens and over every living thing that moves on the earth." (Gen. 1:28)

Our calling to have dominion is a calling to rule, control, and govern.[9] The language of ruling and reigning ought to conjure up images of royalty, of kings and queens ruling over a kingdom. One of the primary ways we bear the image of God is by working. Working is part of God's original design for what it means to be human. Pastor Tim Keller says:

> The mandate to "rule" shows that this act of ruling is a defining aspect of what it means to be made in God's image. We are called to stand in for God here in the world, exercising stewardship over the rest of creation in his place as his vice-regents. We share in doing the things God has done in creation—bringing order out of chaos, creatively building civilizations out of the material of physical and human nature, caring for all that God has made.[10]

God's creation is called to bear witness to its Creator by working.

The Fall

In Genesis 3, sin entered the world when Adam and Eve disobeyed God's commandment not to eat from the Tree of Knowledge of Good and Evil. In an instant, "the human race fell from righteousness to condemnation."[11] Sin marred everything—our relationship with the Lord, relationships with each other, with creation, and of course, our relationship with work. God pronounced judgment upon Adam and Eve. Women would have pain in childbearing, and the relationship between men and women will be marred by struggle. Man's judgment involved his relationship with the "very ground from which he was formed."[12] But God, being rich in mercy, promised the hope of a Savior in Genesis 3:15. In the midst of His judgment, God also promises redemption and restoration through a woman giving birth to a serpent-crushing Son.

We all struggle daily with sin and temptation, as we navigate sorrow and suffering, death and disease, loss and lament. Our work is not immune to sin. We are broken people, working alongside those who hurt and betray us, and within shattered systems, institutions, and organizations.

The Gospel Changes Everything

The good news is that sin, sorrow, and struggle don't have the final word. As we saw in Genesis, God offers humanity the promise of a Savior. All Scripture is telling the story of God's rescuing and redeeming plan for His people through the death, burial, and resurrection of His Son, Jesus. Our sin is paid for, our salvation is secure, and we are called to walk in the Spirit. Just as the impacts of sin are far-reaching, so is the gospel. Christ didn't come just to secure our eternal salvation, but to mold us into His likeness. And for His children to be agents of truth, goodness, and beauty in the world.

The good news of the gospel means that the Lord is redeeming all things to Himself—including work.

To understand the purpose of our work, living in a post-fall world, we must understand it through the lens of the gospel. Tim Keller writes:

> The Christian Gospel is that I am so flawed that Jesus had to die for me, yet I am so loved and valued that Jesus was glad to die for me. This leads to deep humility and deep confidence at the same time. It undermines both swaggering and sniveling. I cannot feel superior to anyone, and yet I have nothing to prove to anyone. I do not think more of myself nor less of myself. Instead, I think of myself less.[13]

Our identity as redeemed children of the Most High has significance for *how* and *why* we work. No longer are we working for our own advancement, achievement, glory, or fame. We aren't working simply for a paycheck. When connected to the bigger picture of what God is up to, all our work can have deep significance, both now and for eternity.

As we allow the truths of the gospel to seep into our souls and reorient our lives, we'll be daily reminded that the crux of the gospel is the fact that we cannot work for our salvation. Jesus accomplished what we could not accomplish—payment for our sins. Jesus' actions on our behalf allow us to rest eternally secure. We are now free to joyfully serve both God and neighbor, resting in the fact that we are forgiven and freed from the crushing burden of guilt and shame.

- The gospel reminds us that we don't need to hustle for approval or significance. We already have all we need for life and godliness.

- The gospel frees us up from solely pursuing worldly success but calls us to a life of holiness and faithfulness.
- The gospel tells us that we can rest in Him because the greatest work has already been finished.
- The gospel says that our worth doesn't come from our work.

In 2 Corinthians, we're reminded that in Christ, we are a new creation, and that "God . . . through Christ reconciled us to himself and gave us the ministry of reconciliation."[14] Jeff Haanen, the founder of the Denver Institute for Faith and Work, says that "God is reconciling the world to himself in Christ, which includes individuals, communities, and entire cities. *Work is our chance* to participate in His redemption of *all things*."[15] Our work is one of the primary avenues through which we love our neighbor and tell the world about what God is like.

While we can take deep pleasure and satisfaction from our work, we must remember that work isn't ultimate. The Holy Spirit is actively working in our hearts to rid us of our idols and reorient our gaze on Jesus. Our identity is no longer directly connected to our roles, but our identity is found in being God's children. When we remember that work is so much bigger than ourselves, we will spend time thinking and dreaming about how our work might help others flourish and how we might love our neighbor through our work. We work hard and with excellence, while simultaneously joyfully resting in Christ's saving work for us.

CALLED TO CULTIVATE

The creation mandate God entrusted to Adam and Eve was a calling to cultivate. We see echoes of this calling throughout Scripture, and the calling extends to us today. The word *cultivate* means to "take steps to grow or improve something,"[16] and can be applied to relationships, skills, cultures, etc. When we engage in the work of cultivation, we are helping *something* or *someone* to flourish. This call to cultivation doesn't mean that you must change the world, solve every injustice, write a bestselling novel, run for office, or start a nonprofit. In essence, this calling to cultivate is a call to faithfulness.

- When a teacher is instructing a classroom, she's cultivating young minds.
- When a doctor is treating patients, she's cultivating those who need physical healing.
- When a policymaker advances a piece of legislation, she is cultivating a certain aspect of society.
- When a mother is changing her baby's diaper or reading her toddler a story, she is cultivating the life of her child.
- When you load the dishwasher, you're cultivating by keeping a clean and inviting household.
- When you show up to a meeting on time and well prepared, you're cultivating by respecting your coworkers and honoring your commitments.

Each one of these actions matters, both for today and for eternity. God has called us to work, and He cares deeply about the details of our lives. Our work can be infused with eternal meaning and significance. We can rejoice, as Bible teacher Melissa Kruger reminds us, "not because of all you've accomplished, but because your name is written in heaven."[17] When we're able to connect our daily work to what the Lord is doing in the world, our work will have meaning and purpose, even on our hardest and most unsatisfying days. Wherever you find yourself, I want to remind you that the Lord sees you and loves you. It might feel like you're working in obscurity, or like your work doesn't matter, but as God's child, you are never alone in your work. The Lord has promised never to leave or forsake you, no matter how challenging and overwhelming life feels.

CONCLUSION

My desire for this book is to honor women in many different seasons of life, serving in different roles and capacities. God calls each one of us to different roles, assignments, and seasons throughout our lives. Perhaps your current season is a stay-at-home mother of little ones, working full time outside the home . . . or you're trying to balance a combination of the two. Your work matters to God because He has created you to work, called you to rule and reign, and promised to be present in each moment of your life.

With that, let's get to work.

REFLECTION QUESTIONS

How does the truth of the *imago Dei* change how I think about work?

Have I been tempted to reject God's call to reflect Him in my gendered humanity?

How have I been tempted to view work in a way that's unbiblical?

What are some ways the gospel changes how I approach my work?

FURTHER READING

Every Good Endeavor: Connecting Your Work to God's Work—Timothy Keller[18]

SCRIPTURE TO MEDITATE UPON

"Then God said, 'Let us make man in our image, after our likeness. And let them have dominion over the fish of the sea and over the birds of the heavens and over the livestock and over all the earth and over every creeping thing that creeps on the earth.'

So, God created man in his own image,
in the image of God he created him;
male and female he created them.

And God blessed them. And God said to them, 'Be fruitful and multiply and fill the earth and subdue it, and have dominion over the fish of the sea and over the birds of the heavens and over every living thing that moves on the earth.'"

—*Gen. 1:26–28*

Chapter 2

Biblical Patterns for Women and Work

Women's Work Matters in the Kingdom of God

When the value of women is rightly seen and celebrated, their Creator is honored and glorified.

Elyse Fitzpatrick[1]

Women in the US and around the world have been mistreated, undervalued, objectified, silenced, abused, and discriminated against, simply because they are women. The #MeToo movement played out in Hollywood, politics, professional sports, media, and yes, even the church. Our society is deeply misguided and confused about issues of gender and sexuality. No longer can we even collectively agree on what a biological woman is. Gender has become something that people attempt to change through clothes, hormones, and surgery.

To truly unpack the topic of women and work, we must first understand what it truly means to be a woman. Elisabeth Elliot famously said that "the fact that I am a woman does not make me a different kind of Christian, but the fact that I am a Christian makes me a different kind of woman."[2] Scripture richly addresses our womanhood. When we grasp the deep value and importance that God has given to women, it will propel us to become different kinds of women.

THE BIBLE AND WOMEN

Created in His Image

Men and women both have intrinsic value because God created us in *His own image and likeness.*[3] In their phenomenal book *Worthy*, Elyse Fitzpatrick and Eric Schumacher write that "the Bible speaks consistently of God's valuing of women. We see this in the crucial and indispensable role they play throughout redemptive history, from Genesis to Revelation."[4] Women aren't an afterthought in Scripture or in the kingdom of God.

God's creation was incomplete without women. Scripture says that it wasn't good for man to be alone. After Adam named all the animals, there wasn't a helper fit for him.[5] So God put Adam to sleep and created a woman. When Adam saw Eve, he erupted into poetry, delighting in the woman God had made.

> "Bone of my bones
>   and flesh of my flesh;
> she shall be called Woman,
>   because she was taken out of Man." (Gen. 2:23)

Adam celebrates, because at last, he's found one like himself. As Bible teacher Jen Wilkin writes:

> The Bible's first word on man and woman is not what separates them, *but what unites them.* It is a celebration of compatibility, of shared humanness. . . . [Scripture] teaches that both man and woman are from the same garden, created by and in the image of the same God, sharing a physical, mental and spiritual sameness that unites the two of them in a way they cannot be united to anything else in creation.[6] (emphasis mine)

Yet, in many of the sermons or discussions about men and women that I've heard, the conversation immediately begins with men and women's differences. We're told that "men are from Mars, women are from Venus" and that "men are like waffles" and "women are like spaghetti." The explicit message is that we are literally worlds apart from one another. While there are certainly distinctions between men and women and their created roles, we must begin where the Bible begins—*with sameness.*

Created as Ezers

When God created men and women, He declared them both to be *very good.* He also created humanity to be gendered. Both genders possess intrinsic dignity, worth, and value. This fundamental truth about humanity has implications for all areas of life. While God chose for His image to be reflected by both men and women, we are also called to reflect Him in our gendered humanity. Women uniquely resemble God to the world as we steward our authority and callings.

The Hebrew word used in Genesis to describe Eve is *ezer*, and it's the very same term used to describe God's own character in the Psalms.[7] This term is used to signify strength or power and occurs twenty-one times in the Old Testament. The first two times *ezer* is used in Scripture, it's to describe a woman, and the rest of the time, it's used to describe God's character and the way He interacts with His people.

Here are a few examples from Psalms:

> "May he send you ***help*** from the sanctuary and give you support from Zion!" (Ps. 20:2)
>
> "Our soul waits for the Lord; he is our ***help*** and our shield." (Ps. 33:20)

> "But I am poor and needy; hasten to me, O God! You are my ***help*** and my deliverer; O LORD, do not delay!" (Ps. 70:5)
>
> "O Israel, trust in the LORD! He is their ***help*** and their shield." (Ps. 115:9)
>
> "I lift up my eyes to the hills. From where does my ***help*** come? My ***help*** comes from the LORD, who made heaven and earth." (Ps. 121:1–2)

Women were created not only to be warriors but also to be a fortress. We are designed to be a safe place, a shield, a help, and a comfort. When we're modeling these characteristics, we're saying something about who God is and what He is like. These characteristics even manifest themselves in our bodies, during pregnancy but also in the marriage relationship. God crafted a woman's body and spirit to reflect Him in such a powerful way.

If we're honest, many of us might bristle at the term "helper," because without properly understanding the term, it might cause women to feel inferior to men. There have certainly been people who have misapplied this teaching to subjugate women in a way that Scripture never intended. But when we grasp the beauty of our design, it's truly striking. Womanhood is a good gift from God.

Our womanhood, properly understood, is a vital part of who we are as image bearers.

Understanding what the Bible says about women lays the foundation for everything else in life. Scripture is clear on God's care for women, His calling to women, and the role women play in advancing the kingdom of God. We shouldn't shed our femininity at the door of the workplace, but rather understand what it means to be fully female in every sphere of life. Each one of us is created by God, with unique stories, callings, passions, and desires. The roles and work God calls us into will be different, at different seasons in our lives. Instead of trying to cram one another into what we think is the right and proper way to live out our womanhood, let's be the first ones to extend grace and love to one another.

THE VALUE OF WOMEN

God's original design of women was *good*, but Genesis 3 tells us that the fall mars all of creation. In God's kindness, He still uses both men and women to accomplish His good purposes. Throughout Scripture, including the Old Testament, we see the importance and value of women. God uses the lives of women like Rahab, Ruth, Tamar, Bathsheba, Elizabeth, Anna, and Mary in redemptive history. But if we dig even deeper, Scripture clearly communicates the worth of women. Below is a sampling of some of the ways women played an integral role in Scripture:

> The first thing declared "not good" in creation is the lack of a woman. (Gen. 2:18)
>
> The first recorded song in human history is the man rejoicing over the woman. (Gen. 2:23)
>
> A woman will give birth to the Messiah. (Gen. 3:15)
>
> Eve is the first person recorded to speak the name "Yahweh." (Gen. 4:1)
>
> The first recorded appearance of the angel of the Lord is to a woman, Hagar. (Gen. 16:7)
>
> The first person in the Old Testament to bestow a name on God, "the God who sees," is Hagar. (Gen. 16:13)

> The first person to "inquire of the Lord" was Rebekah, and the first declaration of unconditional election was made to her. (Gen. 25:22–23; Rom. 9:10–12)
>
> The first person recorded to dance in worship is a woman, Miriam. (Ex. 15:20–21)
>
> The first person recorded to speak the divine title "Lord of hosts" is a woman, Hannah. (1 Sam. 1:11)
>
> The faith and help of a woman, Rahab, was pivotal in the conquest of Jericho, and the Messiah was one of Rahab's direct descendants. (Matt. 1:5)[8]

While Scripture tells the story of the important role women played in the Old Testament, and how God valued them, the ancient world did not honor or value women. But Jesus, in the New Testament, changed everything for women.

JESUS AND WOMEN

In the Gospels, we see Jesus interacting with, caring for, and relating to all types of women. Jewish and Gentile. Old and young. Virgins and prostitutes. His interactions with women crossed ethnic and cultural lines and demonstrated how He valued them. He interacted with women as rational people, not as inferior, even though the ancient world's treatment of male and female was unequal.

Jesus enjoyed a deep friendship with Mary and Martha, He honored and took care of His mother, and He healed women's physical bodies and met their greatest spiritual needs. But perhaps the most revolutionary way women are woven into the New Testament is their presence at the death, burial, and resurrection of Jesus.

Women were the last to stay with Jesus at the cross, along with one disciple, John. (John 19:25)

A woman is the final person Jesus directly ministered to before his death. (John 19:26–27)

Women were the first tasked with proclaiming news of the resurrection. (Matt. 28:7)

A woman is the first to see the resurrected Lord, and also the first to touch his resurrected body. (Matt. 28:9; John 20:14)

A woman is the first to hear the resurrected Lord's voice—and the first name he utters is a woman's. (John 20:14–18)[9]

The inclusion of women throughout the Old Testament and Jesus' life and ministry should remind us that we have value and significance in the kingdom of God. We remember that our sympathizing Savior cares deeply for women.

Women are created in God's image, and as Christians, we are being conformed to the image of Jesus.[10]

A WOMAN'S HIGHEST CALLING

Perhaps you've been told that a woman's highest calling is to be a wife and mother. While those are good, God-designed roles, they weren't ever meant to be a woman's highest or truest calling. One of the reasons is because God doesn't call every woman into those roles. Single and childless women matter just as much in God's kingdom as wives and mothers. Our callings are larger than our roles because God's calling to Christians applies to every Christian, everywhere, always.

The Great Commission and the Great Commandment are a woman's highest calling.[11]

While our seasons of life fluctuate, the roles we step into and out of change, and we navigate happiness and hardship, what doesn't change is that each of us is valuable in the kingdom of God.

In my book *Longing for Motherhood*, one of my goals was to give the church a more holistic understanding of womanhood. I was born with a somewhat rare medical diagnosis that prevents me from bearing biological children. For years, I deeply wrestled with what it meant to be a woman, if I couldn't bear babies. While it's true that God originally designed women's bodies with the capacity to bear children, we live in a fallen world. Many of you have lost babies through miscarriage, struggled month after month to conceive, navigated difficult relationships with your own mothers, been the target of maliciousness or bullying from other women, or been sexually abused or harassed.

Developing a robust understanding of true biblical womanhood helps us establish a solid framework and foundation through which we filter everything about our lives. This helps us navigate questions relating to our individual assignments, how to wisely steward our current season of life, and how to best serve our families, communities, churches, and society.

Women are a vital part of the flourishing of the church, the flourishing of society, and the flourishing of the family.

BIBLICAL PATTERNS FOR WOMEN AND WORK

With a robust understanding of the Lord's intimate care for women and the importance of women in the kingdom of God, we can now turn our attention and focus to what the Bible says about women and work.

Proverbs 31 is the quintessential passage for a holistic model of a godly woman. This passage of Scripture is a poem written by King Lemuel, based on lessons that his mother taught him. She teaches him how to properly conduct himself as king and how to pursue justice and righteousness, and it is, of course, a picture of a woman who fears the Lord. Proverbs 31 tells us that "a woman who fears the LORD is to be praised," but also touches on multiple life domains—family, vocation, and service. This passage tells us the story of a working woman and gives us a wonderful model for *how* and *why* we work. She works hard, not for personal gain, but for the good of her household and the good of others. Below, Scripture tells us how the Proverbs 31 woman works. This passage can offer us wisdom for how we approach our vocations:

> She *seeks* wool and flax, she *works* with willing hands . . . she *rises* while it is yet night and *provides* food for her household . . . she *considers* a field and buys it; with the *fruit of her hands* she plants a vineyard. She *dresses herself with strength* and makes her arms strong . . . she *opens her hand* to the poor and . . . needy.[12]

In the New Testament, we learn that Paul was supported by women like Lydia and Phoebe. He believed that these women "who worked outside their homes, were a great benefit to him and to the gospel. They were to use their careers, whether in the home or the marketplace, in service of the Great Commission, and they were to rest in the truth that whatever way they chose to witness for him, the Lord would be with them."[13] Women and their contributions, callings, and vocations are significant in the kingdom of God and advancing the flourishing of others.

WOMEN AND WORK

The Impact of Women Throughout History

Throughout history, women have helped change the world. At just twenty-eight years old, Amy Carmichael went to India as a missionary. During her time in India, she not only shared the good news of the gospel, she also rescued over a thousand young Indian girls from being temple prostitutes and cared for them. Florence Nightingale was known as the founder of modern nursing, and she spent her days caring for the sick and the vulnerable. Sojourner Truth was an outspoken advocate for abolition, temperance, and civil and women's rights in the nineteenth century.

While we know the names and stories of some of the women who impacted their communities and society, there are countless women whose work history has not remembered. But the Lord saw and knew. Our work doesn't have to be flashy, in the public eye, or even remembered to have an impact on the world around us. Our quiet acts of love and service, done for God's glory, will have reverberations throughout eternity.

Our Current Moment

One question we must ask is how we rightly apply God's Word to our lives, in this current moment. We have been called to live in a particular time in history, in a particular place, alongside particular people. Being a working *woman* means that our calculations and considerations are different from men. Each of us must make wise decisions about working outside the home, stepping back for a season to raise children or care for elderly parents, shifting to a job that allows for greater flexibility, and shifting to part-time work, etc. Our individual callings, capacities, giftings, seasons, and communities will require each one of us to make thoughtful choices about our work.

To understand our current moment in regard to women and the workplace, it's important to examine a brief history of women in the workplace. The Industrial Revolution and the invention of the internet caused two of the largest shifts in how humans work in the past five hundred years. As Andy Crouch says, "the world that the Industrial Revolution gave us . . . was a radical, dramatic transformation in what it means to be human."[14] It transformed rural societies into industrialized, urban ones. Additionally, the advent of the internet and smartphones fundamentally shifted humanity, and our approach to work. Before, during, and after those two major shifts in work and society, there were milestones for women and work.

Brief Timeline of Women and Work

1769: The thirteen colonies prevented women from owning property[15]

1869: First female lawyer in the US[16]

1873: The US Supreme Court ruled that Illinois could exclude women from practicing law[17]

1889: Anna Bissell becomes first female CEO[18]

1912: Massachusetts sets first minimum wage for women[19]

1917: Jeannette Rankin of Montana is the first woman to serve in Congress[20]

1920: The passage of the 19th Amendment grants women the right to vote[21]

1933: Frances Perkins becomes first female Secretary of Labor[22]

1945: The female labor force grew by 50 percent during World War II, as approximately 6.7 million women were added to the workforce[23]

1963: Equal Pay Act prohibits sex-based wage discrimination between men and women[24]

1964: Civil Rights Act prohibits employers from discriminating against workers on the basis of sex, along with race, religion, and national origin[25]

1971: The US Supreme Court outlawed the practice of private employers refusing to hire women with preschool-aged children[26]

1972: Title IX prohibits sex discrimination in any education program or activity receiving federal financial assistance[27]

1972: Katherine Graham was named CEO of *The Washington Post* and became the first female CEO of a Fortune 500 company[28]

1978: Congress passes the Pregnancy Discrimination Act, which bans employers from discriminating on the basis of pregnancy[29]

1981: Sandra Day O'Connor becomes first woman on the Supreme Court[30]

1983: Sally Ride becomes the first American woman astronaut to travel to space[31]

1986: The US Supreme Court rules that "severe or pervasive" sexual harassment of an employee by their supervisor violates federal law[32]

1988: Congress passed the Women's Business Ownership Act, which eliminated a requirement for women to have a male cosigner on a business loan[33]

1993: Congress passed the Family and Medical Leave Act, which helped make it easier for women to balance work and family needs. The law grants eligible workers up to twelve weeks of unpaid time off each year for pregnancy, care of a newborn, adoption or foster care, and other caretaking duties.

1998: The US Supreme Court ruled that employers are now liable for sexual harassment from supervisors[34]

2010: Congress amended the Fair Labor Standards Act to include a provision ensuring that nursing mothers received mandatory break time[35]

All of this brings us to our current moment. Work has even changed since I began writing this book. The COVID-19 pandemic dramatically shifted the way we work. Some of us were laid off, others worked much longer hours (frontline workers). Many of us navigated working from home while trying to facilitate remote learning with children. Some of us got sick, some of us lost loved ones, and some are walking through the symptoms of long COVID that affect our daily lives.

While work will continue changing and evolving as new technologies and policies are introduced, what will never change is our calling to glorify the Lord with the totality of our lives, in whatever season we find ourselves in. Women have a vital role to play in work, whether inside the home, outside the home, or a combination of the two. Let us remember that our highest calling is to glorify the Lord and love our neighbor.

REFLECTION QUESTIONS

Have you been tempted to believe that a woman's highest calling is to be a wife and mother?

How can you help remind others that a woman's highest calling is to fulfill the Great Commandment and the Great Commission?

What stood out to you the most about the history of women and work?

FURTHER READING

Worthy: Celebrating the Value of Women—
Elyse Fitzpatrick and Eric Schumacher[36]

SCRIPTURE TO MEDITATE UPON

"So God created man in his own image, in the image of God he created him; male and female he created them."

—*Gen. 1:27*

"She seeks wool and flax, and works with willing hands. She is like the ships of the merchant; she brings her food from afar. She rises while it is yet night and provides food for her household and portions for her maidens. She considers a field and buys it; with the fruit of her hands she plants a vineyard. She dresses herself with strength and makes her arms strong. She perceives that her merchandise is profitable. Her lamp does not go out at night. She puts her hands to the distaff, and her hands hold the spindle. She opens her hand to the poor and reaches out her hands to the needy."

—*Prov. 31:13–20*

Chapter 3

Approaching Our Work as Christians

Scripture Offers Us a Better Way to Work

"Well done, good and faithful servant. You have been faithful over a little; I will set you over much. Enter into the joy of your master."

Matthew 25:23

After my boss on Capitol Hill resigned, the staff had limited time before the new member of Congress came in and our jobs ended. The days dwindled, and I still didn't have anything lined up. I'd started my career on Capitol Hill as a scheduler and was in that role for a few years before I moved into policy. Organization and scheduling come naturally to me, so I decided to apply for some executive assistant roles, alongside some policy positions. Even though I'd applied to multiple places, the hiring process for the policy jobs I was interested in was taking longer than I could afford to wait. I was offered a job at a law firm as an executive assistant, and with just a few days before our paychecks ended, I took the role, even though it wasn't my first choice.

When I took the job at the law firm, my husband and I had been married for less than a year, and *Longing for Motherhood* had released a few months earlier. Exhaustion and weariness from the transitions set in, and I began the job with a less-than-stellar attitude. Washington, DC, is one of the most expensive places to live in the United States, and I didn't have the luxury of taking more time to job search because I needed to financially contribute to our family during that season. My days were bookended with a complaining tongue and a frustrated heart. My husband would be on the receiving end of my complaints at the end of the day as I processed the professional disappointment I faced.

As I sat on the thirty-minute bus ride downtown to work, one of the questions I frequently mulled over was how the Lord was redeeming and caring for me in a job I didn't enjoy, especially after I'd been at a job where I found deep satisfaction, purpose, and meaning. I wrestled with other questions, such as:

Was the Lord still working for my good in a job I didn't enjoy?

Did God care about my professional life?

How did I honor the Lord in a job I wasn't thrilled about?

How could the Lord use me in this job, as I processed my difficult job loss?

In short, the question I was asking was: *How does God redeem work?*

Of course, I was also processing suddenly and publicly losing my job. With my job on the Hill, I'd woken up each morning with a sense of drive and purpose. I was working to advance human flourishing through public policy, and I saw the direct implications of my work when I helped a constituent navigate a tricky situation or helped craft good legislation. No job is perfect, but overall, I thoroughly loved what I did.

The Lord is always working out *all* things for good because He has promised to one day redeem and restore all things.[1] On this side of eternity, we often don't see or understand how or why certain things happen, but we can trust the good character of our God. In the moment of job transition and job loss, I had to wrestle through *how*

He was redeeming the work I didn't enjoy, and how my work helped me love my neighbor, even if I didn't see the direct implications of it.

Alternatively, when I've worked in jobs that I absolutely adore, I've had to wrestle to put work in its proper place and regularly remind my soul that work isn't ultimately about me, but it serves a greater purpose. As I'm writing this chapter, I'm in the midst of another job transition and reminding myself of the truths I've written about. Things I know to be true but can be tempted to forget.

I don't know what your professional life has looked like. Perhaps you've had success after success and haven't encountered much turmoil in your work. But more than likely, your relationship and experience with work has been a mixed bag of joys and struggles as you've sought to navigate working in a modern workforce. I believe all of us have a desire to rightly steward the work we've been entrusted with, and the good news is, our work matters both now and for eternity.

WHAT DOES IT MEAN TO BE A CHRISTIAN AT WORK?

Many of us might wrestle with what it means to be a Christian in the workplace. Does it mean displaying a Bible verse at our workstation and hoping someone notices and asks us about it? Does it mean mentioning church when someone asks about our weekend plans? Is it evangelizing our unsaved coworkers and starting a Bible study over the lunch hour? Does it mean behaving morally and ethically?

While all those things are true of Christians in the workplace, our call as Christians in the workplace is more holistic. Our work *itself* matters to God, and Scripture shapes and changes how and why we work.

A Long Obedience in the Same Direction

In Eugene Peterson's fantastic book *A Long Obedience in the Same Direction*, he discusses the long, hard, and holy work of discipleship.

The call of the Christian life is to commit to a lifetime of faithfully following Jesus. Our long obedience is deeply rooted in the promise that one day all things will be made right. The Lord is going to redeem and restore all things, and sin, strife, and sorrow will be no more. All will be well, because Jesus has promised to prepare a place for us and will return to bring us to Himself where we'll spend eternity with Him.

We have staked our entire life on that promise and cling to it for dear life. As Peterson reminds us, "Hoping does not mean doing nothing. It is not fatalistic resignation. It means going about our assigned tasks, confident that God will provide the meaning and the conclusions. . . . It means a confident, alert expectation that God will do what he said he will do. It is imagination put in the harness of faith. It is a willingness to let God do it his way in his time."[2] Our entire lives become a long obedience, faithfully co-laboring with Christ, as we offer the world a beautiful picture of who God is and what He is like. We work toward renewal and restoration.

Our perspective is no longer solely shaped by what we can see, touch, and feel. No, we are people of the promise, who work to give the world foretastes of eternity with our words and deeds. We are living in the tension of the already and the not yet. God's kingdom "has been inaugurated, but it is yet to be fully consummated."[3] We know that our work matters today, whether feeding a hungry child, writing a persuading article, designing an impactful presentation, or excelling at customer service, but our work also matters for eternity.

As John Mark Comer says, "Our job is to make the invisible God visible—to mirror and mimic what he is like to the world. We can glorify God by doing our work in such a way that we make the invisible God visible by *what we do* and *how we do it*."[4]

As we consider our work, may we allow this verse to strengthen our spirit: "Be steadfast, immovable, always abounding in the work of the Lord, knowing that in the Lord your labor is not in vain" (1 Cor. 15:58). What good news—our labor is not in vain.

HOW SHOULD WE APPROACH OUR WORK?

Ambassadorship

Ambassadors are authorized "messengers or representatives."[5] They are representing their country in a different place, a different kingdom. Ambassadors do not represent themselves, but the one who sent them.

So it is with us.

Scripture tells us that "we are ambassadors for Christ" (2 Cor. 5:20). We represent King Jesus and work as unto Him. Ambassadorship changes everything about how we approach our work. We are free from the motivations that drive nonbelievers in the workplace. Our ultimate aim isn't for power, money, fame, influence, or success. It is to glorify the Lord through word and deed. We can be quick to forgive when a coworker wrongs us because we have been forgiven in Christ. We can hold our professional plans loosely because we trust that the Lord is directing all of our steps. We can work hard and with excellence because we know that our work is not in vain. We are ultimately people of another kingdom, working for our good King.

Stewardship

Our approach to work must also be marked with a posture of stewardship. A steward is one who manages or looks after something that is not their own. Stewards have been entrusted with the responsibility to tend to and care for something that is on loan to them. The idea of stewardship is seen throughout the pages of the Bible and goes back to Genesis 1:28, where God commands Adam and Eve to "rule over the fish in the sea and the birds in the sky and over every living creature that moves on the ground." God's commandment is for His people to rule on His behalf. Everything is ultimately on loan from the Lord; we are temporarily stewarding those resources.

In 1 Corinthians 12, Paul talks about one body having many members. God created each of us with different backgrounds, stories, capacities, giftings, and passions. Each one of us is valuable, and our contributions matter, not only to the local body of believers, but to the work that God has called us to. We have a responsibility to use our gifts and talents for the good of others and not to squander it.

I'll admit that a posture of stewardship doesn't come naturally to me. Ownership and self-sufficiency tend to be my default postures, and I often fail to remember that nothing I have is truly *mine.* Scripture tells me that "it is required of stewards that they be found faithful" (1 Cor. 4:2). A stewardship mindset pries open our death grip on life. Our jobs, our finances, our families, our friends, our influence, our careers, our bodies, our time, and our talents, ultimately, aren't to be used for self-satisfaction and self-fulfillment. But they are to be joyfully given back to the Lord for Him to use for His good purposes—they are His after all.

HOW DOES GOD REDEEM WORK?

Work as Worship

As we adopt the mindset of long obedience, the posture of steward and ambassador, we are now ready to consider how our work itself matters and has meaning. Romans 12:1 connects *all* of life with worship: "I appeal to you therefore, brothers, by the mercies of God, to present your bodies as a living sacrifice, holy and acceptable to God, which is your spiritual worship." Everything in our lives can be an offering to the Lord. What we do with our bodies and our minds is significant to God.

The Hebrew term *avodah* simultaneously means "work, worship, and service."[6] Austin Burkhart says that the first time "avodah" is used is in Genesis 2:15, telling us that "God's original design and desire is that our work and our worship would be a seamless way of living."[7] In some verses, the term "avodah" means work and labor:

> "Six days you shall work [avodah]." (Ex. 34:21)
>
> "Man goes out to his work [avodah] and to his labor until the evening." (Ps. 104:23)

In other verses, "avodah" means worship.

> "Thus says the Lord, 'Let my people go, that they may serve [avodah] me.'" (Ex. 8:1)
>
> "But as for me and my household, we will serve [avodah] the Lord." (Josh. 24:15)

This concept of "avodah" teaches us how to live integrated and congruent lives, where everything we do matters in the kingdom of God. Our work is the means by which we can worship the Lord. So, whether your work is waiting tables, changing diapers, typing reports, leading board meetings, advocating for change, or composing music, may all of it be an offering to the Lord. He's present with us in our work and desires for every area of our lives to be used in worship to Him.

Work as a Way to Love Our Neighbor

Martin Luther once said that "God does not need our good works, but our neighbor does."[8]

Work is not only a wonderful way to worship God; it is one of the ways through which we love our neighbor. The gospel reshapes our hearts so that our work is not for selfish gain or self-actualization but is neighbor-focused. We are a redeemed people, and our good works flow from forgiven hearts.

Love, in the Christian sense, is not *only* an emotion. C. S. Lewis reminds us that "it is a state . . . of the will; that state of the will which we have naturally about ourselves and must learn to have about other people." He goes on to offer us this counsel, "Do not waste time bothering whether you 'love' your neighbor; act as if you did. As soon as we do this, we find one of the great secrets. When you are behaving as if you loved someone, you will presently come to love him."[9] Even if we don't feel great emotional affection for our customers or our coworkers, we can still choose to obey the commandment to love and serve our neighbors through our work.

Consider what it looks like for your work to love your neighbor and advance human flourishing. Tim Keller says that "work is a major instrument of God's providence; it is how he sustains the human world."[10] When we work, we help communities, society, and the world thrive. A useful question to ponder is, "How does my work help my neighbor to flourish?" With some jobs, it's easy to draw a direct line from your work to human flourishing. But maybe you don't immediately grasp how your work is directly impacting the world. In that case, consider how the world would be different without your work.

I'm writing this chapter in a local coffee shop, sipping on a cinnamon oat latte. For this pleasant afternoon to occur, someone had to work to open a coffee shop, and the baristas had to learn their craft. But digging even deeper, someone had to make the individual components of my drink—oat milk, cinnamon, espresso. And then people worked to ship them to this coffee shop. By purchasing this cup of coffee, I'm also helping support a local business and encourage ethical business practices. I'm also writing this book on a computer, built with the expertise and talent of hundreds of people. Each one of the engineers and designers has a skill that would take me a lifetime to begin to attempt to learn. But they intimately know their craft, and because of their hard work designing a computer, I can now sit and fill blank pages with words. Because of their creation, I can now create.

Work, by its very nature, touches the lives of others—whether you're healing patients as a medical professional, forming minds in the classroom, coaching others on how to create a successful business, helping others do their taxes, or cleaning houses. Each one of us has a role to play. Our work helps the world to function and flourish.

For every job, you must give thought to how your work helps or harms your neighbor. The Center for Faith and Work, started by Timothy Keller and Katherine Leary Alsdorf, helps Christians "explore and investigate the gospel's unique power to renew hearts, communities, and the world, in and through day-to-day work."[11] They provide some helpful questions to ask, as you examine the industry or sphere you serve in:

- How are things in this sphere supposed to be (as created by God)?
- How are things in this sphere going wrong (because of systemic evil)?
- How might God be calling me/us to join him in the redemption and renewal of this particular sphere?[12]

Take time to prayerfully work through those questions and explore how the work you do is connected to the bigger picture. God redeems work when we offer it up to Him as an act of worship and use it as a way to love our neighbor.

Sharing the Gospel at Work

As Christians, we are called to share the good news of the gospel faithfully and regularly (Mark 16:15). But for many of us, sharing the gospel with our coworkers can feel intimidating.

What if they don't respond well?

What if they make fun of me behind my back?

What if this changes our relationship?

In their book *The Gospel at Work*, Sebastian Traeger and Greg Gilbert offer excellent suggestions for how to share the gospel in the workplace. One of their suggestions is to build relationships with your coworkers.[13]

At the law firm, I was the only Christian in my immediate circle of colleagues. As I built trust and relationships with my coworkers, I began sharing pieces of myself and my story with them. It took time to build and deepen these relationships. Intentional relationship building usually occurred over morning walks to the local coffee shop or over lunches. I wanted my colleagues to know that I valued them not only as coworkers, but holistically as people. To build these types of relationships with your coworkers, show a genuine interest in them.

Know when it's appropriate to have these types of conversations. The Free Exercise Clause of the US Constitution protects the right of Americans to believe and practice their faith.[14] However, businesses have the ability to restrict employee behavior during work hours. To avoid any issues, it's best to use company time to do what you are hired and paid to do—your job. You can build relationships with your colleagues and share your faith off the clock. For example, as I got to know my coworkers, I began to share the hope of the gospel with them. These conversations would happen during coffee and lunch breaks, or after work, as we were walking to the bus together. While some coworkers have been more open to the gospel than others, in all the places I've worked, people knew I was a Christian. My desire was for them to know that I was always available to have conversations about faith, pray for them, or just be a listening ear in a difficult season.

Traeger and Gilbert also suggest "learning to put God on the table."

> Let people know in natural, easygoing, confident ways that you're a Christian. . . . When someone asks what you did over the weekend, tell them you went to church. Mention

> the Bible study you attend on Tuesday nights. Don't just mumble, "I'm sorry I can't come to your birthday party; I'm busy." Say, "I can't come because I'm scheduled to work at my church's clothes closet this weekend." You don't have to be obnoxious or irresponsible about it. Just make sure you identify yourself publicly with Jesus. Let people know somehow you're a Christian and don't mentally censor your Christianity out of your interactions and conversations. You'll be amazed at how often people will take the opportunity to press in on the little piece of information you've just offered. People are often more interested in spiritual things than you think. They just need a bit of permission from you to feel free to talk about it.[15]

These suggestions are so practical and open the door to more in-depth conversations about why you believe what you believe. Building relationships with coworkers in a remote work environment can be a bit more challenging, but certainly not impossible. Don't give yourself a pass just because you're a remote employee. You'll have to be more intentional and take more initiative to create trusted relationships with those you regularly interact with through a Zoom call.

What do you do if you work for yourself, or work for a church or Christian ministry and don't regularly interact professionally with non-Christians? Build intentional rhythms into your life for opportunities to interact with nonbelievers. Perhaps you go to the same coffee shop a few times a week and build a relationship with your local baristas. Perhaps you take your children to the local playground and build relationships with other parents as your children play together. Ask the Lord for opportunities to regularly share the gospel, and for eyes to see those opportunities.

Well Done, Good and Faithful Servant

The good news of the gospel is that our work *does* matter. It matters because the Lord has called us to work, to worship, and to love our neighbor. He promises that nothing done for Him is ever in vain.

In Jesus' parable of the talents, He tells the story of two servants who faithfully stewarded what they'd been entrusted with. Their master praised them and said, "Well done, good and faithful servant. You have been faithful over a little; I will set you over much. Enter into the joy of your master" (Matt. 25:23). Each of us should long to hear that praise from Jesus at the end of our lives.

The Lord doesn't say, well done, good and faithful CEO, manager, or employee. He says, "Well done, good and faithful *servant*." As we work, may we remember that being a faithful servant of our Master is the main aim and goal of our lives, and may everything we do come from an overflow of His great love for us. May we walk in a manner worthy of our calling, as God's beloved children, as we work with diligence, creativity, passion, and excellence. May we faithfully strive to please an audience of one, first and foremost.

The liturgy for the midday hours from *Every Moment Holy* is one I read often, because it helps me quickly reorient my heart in the middle of my days. I'd like to end this chapter with this short prayer.

> We labor, O Lord, as stewards of your creation, and as stewards of the gifts you have apportioned to each of us for the good of all. Bless then the works of our hands and minds and hearts, O God, that they might bear fruit for your greater purposes. May our work this day be rendered first as service to you, that the benefits of it might be eternal.[16]

REFLECTION QUESTIONS

How can I approach my work as a steward?

What are some ways I can regularly remind my soul that my call is first and foremost to faithfulness?

What story am I telling the world about God through my work?

How can I build intentional relationships with colleagues to share the gospel?

FURTHER READING

Visions of Vocation: Common Grace for the Common Good—
Steven Garber[17]

SCRIPTURE TO MEDITATE UPON

"And he said to them, 'Go into all the world and proclaim the gospel to the whole creation.'"

—*Mark 16:15*

"As each has received a gift, use it to serve one another, as good stewards of God's varied grace."

—*1 Peter 4:10*

"And let us not grow weary of doing good, for in due season we will reap, if we do not give up."

—*Gal. 6:9*

Chapter 4

A Season for Everything

How to Live Out Your Assignment from the Lord

"For everything there is a season,
and a time for every purpose under heaven."

Ecclesiastes 3:1

Growing up, I had no clue what I wanted to be. My father was an architect, and I thought I might want to do that, until I realized that I hated math, engineering, and the skills needed to pursue that career path. I didn't formally declare my major in college until my junior year because I wasn't quite sure which major was right for me. I tried on majors like hats, before finally squeezing by with my degree in international relations. In college, I knew I wanted to move overseas but wasn't sure which degree would get me there. When the Lord redirected my steps and I moved to Washington, DC, I still wasn't sure how to use my degree and my experiences.

Whenever I've met with younger people who are interested in pursuing a career in policy and advocacy, like the one I have, or in writing publicly, their number one question has been, "How did you do it?" What they are looking for is the secret sauce to securing a similar career. And while there is a lot of wisdom in seeking career guidance, the reality is two people could have the same job or reach the same level of leadership, but their paths could be completely different.

I used to be envious of people who appeared to know exactly what they wanted to do. But for most of us, our professional journeys often include paying attention to how God has equipped us and figuring out how our interests and desires could lead to a career. My first job in DC was at a nonprofit doing grassroots work. I quickly learned that I didn't enjoy my work. While I appreciated the mission of the organization, the tasks that filled my day were tedious and difficult for me. My heart lit on fire with public policy, especially policy issues surrounding human rights and the vulnerable. So, I started keeping my ears open for different roles. I didn't want to change jobs carelessly but wanted my next move to be closer aligned to work that was meaningful to me. The opportunity came to be a scheduler on Capitol Hill for a congressman that I deeply respected. Even though I didn't want to be a scheduler forever, I immediately took the job because it got me closer to what I wanted to do.

Whenever someone asks me how I've gotten to do the work I've done, whether it's working in policy and advocacy, writing opinion pieces, or even writing books, I always tell them that there's no linear path. In fact, many moments in my career have felt like I've taken a few steps backward, or away, from where I thought I should be. People don't often see the long hours of writing at 5:00 a.m. before I head to my nine-to-five job. They aren't aware of all the heartache and turmoil I've walked through, as two bosses I've worked under have resigned (albeit, for very different reasons), or the dozens of books, articles, and white papers I've read to develop and sharpen my skill set.

My generation was told that we could be anything we want to be, but that comes at a cost because few of us actually know *what* we want to be. Some of you do, and that's a beautiful thing. But for those of us who don't quite know how we should spend our life, there's good news.

CALLING VS. ASSIGNMENT

Maybe you've been told that you need to figure out your calling to live a fulfilled life. A quick Google search on "finding your calling" brings up the following:

- How to Find Your Calling: 5 Ways to Discover What You Were Born to Do
- How to Find Your Calling from God: 6 Steps to Find God's Calling in Your Life
- Find Your Calling: 5 Steps to Identify Your Purpose
- 10 Ways to Uncover Your True Calling
- 15 Ways to Find Your Calling in Life for a Meaningful Life

Just reading those headlines makes me exhausted and confused. Do I need twenty ways to find my calling or just five? We don't have to be faced with a haunting fear that our lives won't matter, or we won't live a meaningful life if we don't find our "calling." The good news for us is that Scripture tells us a more beautiful story. Nancy Ray, in a podcast episode on this topic, says there's a difference between our calling and our assignments: "Your calling never changes, but your assignment changes from season to season."[1]

The calling of every Christian is the call to follow Jesus. We can pursue faithful obedience to Christ regardless of our role, circumstance, season of life, or salary. We don't have to wonder about our calling because Christ has told us. We are to love the Lord our God and love our neighbor as ourselves. John Piper reminds us that "the greatest cause in the world is joyfully rescuing people from hell, meeting their earthly needs, making them glad in God, and doing it with a kind, serious pleasure that makes Christ look like the Treasure he is."[2] We can honor and obey this calling whether we're single, married, childless, the mother of multiple children, wealthy, or hardly have two pennies to rub together. This should give us a deep sense of peace and rest. We don't have to panic to find our calling. We are already called, and in that calling, we are deeply loved by our Father. When we're faithfully following Christ, we're fulfilling our calling.

If we are faithfully following Christ by seeking to glorify Him, and love our neighbor, we don't have to worry about missing our calling.

Assignments

Our calling will always remain the same, but our assignments throughout life will change.

An *assignment* is, by definition, a task to which one is assigned.[3] You can be appointed by God to different positions, in different seasons of life. One of the surest things about life is that it's constantly changing. Your assignment right now will likely look different in six months, six years, and two decades.

Throughout our lives, we'll step into different roles and assignments. Some types of roles include friend, daughter, wife, mother, full-time employee, part-time employee, boss, volunteer in the community, serving in the church, grandmother, or caretaker. Your assignments will change throughout your life as well. Sometimes we're in a particular role for the rest of our lives, but some roles are temporary—for example, your season of life with a newborn baby. Babies grow quickly, and soon you'll go from nurturing a newborn to parenting a toddler. Maybe you're in a season where you've stepped back from working outside the home to raise children. Or perhaps you're rethinking some rhythms in your life to help you live more fully into the assignments the Lord has given you and prayerfully considering what adjustments you need to make. Each one of us is living into different assignments, at different times.

How you experience your role during a given season will also change. For example, the first few years of marriage might be difficult, as you learn about and adjust to one another and the new rhythms of life as a couple. After welcoming a child into your family, you might experience postpartum depression. That particular season of motherhood will be different from raising a teenager. You're still a mother, but how you experience your role changes.

As I've written this book, my assignments have shifted. I've stepped into a new role that came with a large learning curve. My husband and I said yes to an adoption match and moved to a new state. Some of my assignments haven't changed. I'm still a wife to my husband, Michael, a daughter to my parents, a sister, and a friend. I'm still a member of a local body of believers, I'm still working full time, and I'm still writing.

Instead of asking, "What is my calling?" a better question to ask yourself is, "What is my current assignment?" God's assignments for your life belong to you and not your neighbor. It's tempting to look at someone else's life and feel like we're behind and we need to catch up. Or to feel envious about what someone's current assignments are and wish they were ours. But consider the assignments you've been entrusted with and seek to honor those assignments.

Seasons of Life

The concept of seasons has deeply resonated with me and been a helpful framework as I've thought through calling and assignments. Think about the physical seasons. As the temperatures drop, the air cools and the leaves begin to change, we pull out cozy blankets and candles to snuggle into the autumn months. Then as the holidays approach, we spruce up the house with twinkle lights, a tree, and touches of red and green. In the spring, as leaves and flowers begin to bud and bloom, we throw open the windows to let the fresh air in.

For the longest time, I despised the long, cold, dark winter months. I grew up in the South and wasn't prepared for more robust winters. Finally, I decided that I wasn't going to be miserable half of the year. Winter comes annually, whether I like it or not, and I committed to lean into the physical seasons of the year instead of wishing them away or longing for another season. Now, I want to press into each physical season and deeply enjoy it because soon it is gone.

The same is true for our seasons of life. Some seasons are easier than others. Some are marked with deep sorrow and pain. Most of our seasons are a mixture of the two, navigating the tension of joy and sorrow. Our professional lives will go through seasons too. Women's participation in the workforce will look different throughout their lives. Very few women experience the career predictability men do. We step back to raise children. We work part time to accommodate different responsibilities. We navigate the tension of our different roles, wanting to do them well. As we walk through the seasons of our life, may we remember that the God of seasons promises never to leave or forsake His children, even in the most difficult and dark seasons.

THE CALL TO FAITHFULNESS

As we're living out our assignments, we must remember that we are called to faithfulness. J. D. Greear writes that "what God requires of you is not success, but faithfulness in what he has assigned to you."[4] He encourages us to ponder the question of what Jesus has called *you* to do and reminds us that we "aren't responsible to save the world, but [we] are responsible to follow Christ in [our] situation."[5] Success, in God's eyes, is faithfully following Him, wherever He calls. This frees us up from feeling like the weight of the world is on our shoulders. We are free to follow God in the ways that He calls us.

Faithfulness doesn't mean that it's wrong to pursue success, excellence, or big dreams about how your work can have great impacts on the world. Rather, faithfulness means that we know how to put those things in their proper place. We work hard and leave the results in the Lord's hands.

Isaiah 49:16 reminds us that we are engraved on the palms of God's hands. God sees and knows His children. Because we are known and loved by God, we are free to joyfully commit to the people and place where the Lord has called us to. We can trust that the work we do matters to God and to others, even if we never see the impact of our work this side of eternity.

Many of our moments and days feel achingly ordinary. We commute, we write emails, we send status updates, we make dinner, we clean the house, build friendships, change a child's diaper . . . and we do it over and over. First Thessalonians 4:11 tells us "to live quietly . . . and to work with your hands." While there are women throughout history who have made dramatic impacts on society and on the world, there are millions of faithful, godly women who have lived quiet lives, diligently loving and serving their families and communities, executing their work with excellence. Their names might not be remembered on earth, but they have received a far better reward than earthly remembrance.

Even if you're in a season where you feel insignificant or unseen, remember that the things that God deems important are often different from what the world values. Sister, press into living a faithful life, no matter what your season of life looks like.

HOW TO STEWARD YOUR VOCATION

The concepts of calling, assignments, and seasons are helpful frameworks, but they don't answer the question of how we're supposed to use the time, talent, and treasure with which the Lord entrusted us.

God gave us specific giftings and passions, but how are we supposed to steward them?

The word "vocation" addresses the wholeness of life. It is a way of being in the world and understanding our relationships and responsibilities. Steven Garber, in his book *Visions of Vocation*, has this to say about vocation:

> It is also true that whether our vocations are as butchers, bakers or candlestick makers—or people drawn into the worlds of business or law, agriculture or education, architecture or construction, journalism or international development, health care or the arts—in our own different ways we are responsible, for love's sake, for the way the world is and ought to be. *We are called to be common grace for the common good.*[6]

Our vocation isn't ultimately about us, but a means by which we can love God and love our neighbor. Because God rules and reigns over *all* creation, that means that what we do on Monday morning is just as important as what we do on Sunday. Therefore, "secular work has no less dignity and nobility than the 'sacred' work of ministry."[7]

How God Has Uniquely Equipped You

Presbyterian theologian Frederick Buechner famously said, "The place God calls you to is the place where your deep gladness and the world's deep hunger meet."[8] Some of you know immediately how your deep gladness and the world's great need intersect. Others of you might not have an immediate answer. I encourage you to prayerfully and thoughtfully explore the questions below. It could be helpful to work through these questions with others who know you well (a spouse, close friend, counselor, or mentor). They'll be able to see things in you that you might not immediately see and to offer helpful feedback and perspective.

- What is my deep gladness?
- What lights up my heart? What issue or topic can I not stop researching, thinking about, or talking about?
- What practical needs does my work help meet?
- How does the world look different because of my work?
- Where are the deep needs in my church, community, and world?
- What do others see in me? What do they believe I'm good at?
- What areas of service bring me joy?

As you work through the questions, you might sense a theme emerging. For example, maybe there's a specific type of work you're drawn to, whether it's a helping profession (social worker, medical professional, teacher), communications (writer, public relations, social media manager), or STEM (science, technology, engineering, and mathematics). Or maybe there's a specific group of people you want to help—refugees, the elderly, children with special needs, businesswomen who need support and encouragement.

For me, child welfare is one of the needs in the world that I care deeply about. I was adopted as an infant from Romania, grew up with five siblings who were adopted, and my husband and I are building our family through adoption. When I worked on Capitol Hill, my boss at the time was the co-chair of the Adoption Caucus, and I was able to cut my teeth on child welfare policy. Currently, my professional role is policy and advocacy for a large organization that cares for vulnerable women, children, and families. The Lord has given me a unique story with adoption, allowed me to develop policy and advocacy skills, and given me opportunities to use both my personal passions and professional skills to help advance the protection and well-being of vulnerable children. Even in seasons where I couldn't professionally work on child welfare issues, I remained involved through volunteer work.

If you're not currently in a job where you feel deep alignment with your skill set and your professional desires, it's okay. Professional congruence is a gift, but not a guarantee. This is where the framing of vocation really matters. Amy Sherman defines the concept of vocational stewardship as "the intentional and strategic deployment of our vocational power—knowledge, platform, networks, position, influence, skills and reputation—to advance foretastes of God's kingdom."[9] We can "seek the well-being of the city"[10] even when our professional lives don't completely match up with our unique giftings and passions. We can volunteer, we can help change company culture, we can use our voices to advocate, and we can start ministries. Committing to the flourishing of our communities will help us to be creative about how we deploy our giftings.

How to Thrive in Your Particular Season

Your season of life is unique to you. No one else has your story, or the specific combination or your personality, passions, and skill set. Throughout life, we make choices great and small that impact our life. We chose to marry *this* person and not that one. We chose *this* neighborhood and not the one across town. We spend our time honing *this* craft and not another one. We should consistently pray for God's wisdom as we seek to steward our lives well. While some decisions have long-term implications, our seasons of life are often changing, even if it's on a micro level. Many of us might feel like as soon as we've found good rhythms for our life something changes, and we're back to square one. The good news is we can thrive in our particular seasons with some forethought and intention.

First, name your season. Are you just starting a new job? That will likely require extra energy as you settle into new professional rhythms, develop new relationships with coworkers, and learn how to successfully execute new responsibilities. Are you transitioning from full-time work to part-time because your children need more of your attention and presence? That will come with its own unique adjustments and learning curve. Is your personal life more demanding than your professional life right now? Are you grieving a deep loss or struggling with depression and anxiety that impacts every area of life, including work? Identifying your season helps you slow down and become more present.

Next, name how this season is impacting you. What are the stressors, demands, joys, and unique challenges of a particular season? From there, you can begin to adjust your life and rhythms to make room for that particular season. Some helpful questions to ask are:

What are the most important priorities in this particular season?
Everything can't be important at once. Especially in very intense seasons, something must give. For example, I'm moving to a new home four days before completing the first draft of this book. The entire month leading up to it has been unusually full and exhausting. Something's had to give, so we've eaten a lot more freezer meals, my workouts have been relatively nonexistent, and I've had to say no to more things than I'd like to be able to focus on the priorities. We aren't able to give equal attention to all parts of our life at once. For example, eating healthy is always valuable because we're caring well for the body God entrusted to us. But in different seasons, we might have to simplify our meals or prioritize spending a little more money on premade healthy meals.

What habits will help me and my family thrive in this particular season?
Justin Whitmel Earley, a Virginia-based attorney, wrote an outstanding book titled *The Common Rule*, in which he discusses habits of

purpose in an age of distraction. I highly commend the entire book to you, but I want to focus on a particular point he makes. He writes that "only when your habits are constructed to match your worldview do you become someone who doesn't just know about God and neighbor but someone who actually loves God and neighbor."[11] Our rhythms will either help us to love God and love our neighbor more or make it more difficult. Spend time evaluating your habits, both individually and as a family. What areas do you need to adjust to be able to spend time with the Lord and with those you love, and to faithfully serve others? Some seasons, your physical and emotional capacity will be smaller than others. As your seasons change, it's helpful to reevaluate your rhythms and adjust as needed.

Benefits of Living Within Our Assigned Seasons

Choosing to live within our own particular season compels us to trust in God's goodness, sovereignty, and power. We trust that we are created by Him for good works and that He is working all things together for good. Yet, many of us tend to operate out of a scarcity mindset, believing there's a finite amount of resources.

- Scarcity says we must grasp every opportunity for dear life.
- Scarcity says there's not enough to go around for everyone.
- Scarcity tells us to be selfish and look out for ourselves first.
- Scarcity tricks us into forgetting that this world is not all there is.

We're constantly bombarded with all that we seemingly lack. We're not fit enough, toned enough, beautiful enough, financially secure enough, or up-to-date with the latest trends. Our house is too small, painted the wrong color, or outdated. We aren't married, we don't have children, we don't have enough children, or our children aren't as well behaved as we'd like them to be. We haven't received that promotion or that raise. We weren't invited to happy hour after work. We're not on the text thread that everyone else in the meeting seems to be on.

The list could go on and on . . .

As we're met with the message of more, our hearts and minds are rewired to think we need to constantly keep up. Yet, Scripture tells us a better story—the story of contentment. Paul writes:

> For I have learned in whatever situation I am to be content. I know how to be brought low, and I know how to abound. In any and every circumstance, I have learned the secret of facing plenty and hunger, abundance and need. I can do all things through him who strengthens me. (Phil. 4:11–13)

This verse has always encouraged me because Paul is communicating that contentment is a learned skill. Contentment takes practice. But the good news is, like Paul, we can learn to be content, no matter what our circumstances are.

- Contentment tells us that we can rest in God's presence and rest within our limitations.
- Contentment reminds us to enjoy what we *do* have, instead of always rushing and clamoring for more.

May we be reminded that our moments, our talents, and our treasure are all a gift from the Lord. Rather than feeling scared because of lack, or always desiring more, may we rest in what God has entrusted to us.

CONCLUSION

Sister, as you press into your season of life, whatever that looks like, remember that you can use all God has entrusted you with to live a life of obedience to the Lord. He has promised to be present with you every step of the journey, and your work is not in vain. I want to leave you with a prayer for vocations from Steven Garber.

> God of heaven and earth, we pray for your kingdom to come, for your will to be done on earth as it is in heaven. Teach us to see our vocations and occupations as woven into your work in the world this week. For mothers at home who care for children for those whose labor forms our common life in this city, the nation and the world, for those who serve the marketplace of ideas and commerce, for those whose creative gifts nourish us all, for those whose callings take them into the academy for those who long for employment that satisfies their souls and serves you, for each one we pray asking for your great mercy. Give us eyes to see that our work is holy to you, O Lord, even as our worship this day is holy to you. In the name of the Father, the Son and the Holy Spirit, Amen.[12]

REFLECTION QUESTIONS

What are some of the current assignments God has entrusted to you?

How can you remember to pursue faithfulness to the Lord above everything else?

What is *most* important for this season of life?

FURTHER READING

Kingdom Calling: Vocational Stewardship for the Common Good—Amy Sherman[13]

SCRIPTURE TO MEDITATE UPON

"For everything there is a season, and a time for every matter under heaven."

—*Eccl. 3:1*

Chapter 5

Dealing with Challenges

How We Fight Sin and Temptation in the Workplace

Sin always begins with the character assassination of God.

Tim Keller[1]

This chapter really needs no introduction because we're all intimately familiar with struggles within the workplace. For many of us, challenges and difficulties are the first thing we think of when work comes to mind. We're all too familiar with the long workdays, the coworkers who get on our nerves, and attempting to "balance" a flourishing family *and* a flourishing career. We know that work is supposed to be an active way to love our neighbor and work toward kingdom advancement, but we often bump up against frustration and incongruence. There's a disconnect between what we know to be true and what we experience.

I've personally experienced many challenges with work, both internal and external, such as struggling with the sin of a prideful heart or gossiping lips. Chances are, you've faced difficulties in your work too, whether it's negotiating a raise, feeling the need to prove yourself to male colleagues, a tendency toward overworking and idolizing work, struggling with laziness, combating feelings of jealousy, unhealthy competition with other women, or placing an unhealthy pressure on yourself to perform. We accidentally hurt one another. Miscommunication and misunderstanding occur. And our gaze may become fixed on competition over competence, or accolades over excellence.

HOW TO NAVIGATE CHALLENGES IN THE WORKPLACE

Because challenges are a part of our daily professional lives, we need to be equipped for how to handle them when they come. Rather than downplaying our struggles, it's important to be honest about the challenges and struggles that we face in our work, so that we can address them and grow. As we navigate temptations that arise in the workplace, it's imperative to have a community of believers who can ask us the difficult questions and hold us accountable. We need to be in communities where we are deeply known, can let our guard down, and can be completely honest with others.

Scripture tells us that we have everything we need for life and godliness, which means Christians have the resources they need to navigate life. While Scripture doesn't offer specific prescriptions for every area of our lives, God does promise that He'll grant us wisdom if we ask Him for it. The first step as we're dealing with work challenges is to ask the Lord for wisdom, repent when we've sinned, and ask for forgiveness from those we've wronged. Work is one of the primary ways we're sanctified because most of us spend the majority of our hours working. Even if you're not working outside the home and you're caring for young children or an aging parent, you're still engaged in work, and you'll face struggles.

WHO WE ARE AT WORK

Whenever we step through the doors of our offices, log on to an online meeting room, sit down to type a report, call a coworker to have a difficult conversation, or file our expenses, we must do so remembering our identity. We must be shaped by who we are in Christ rather than our title, the letters behind our name, or our salaries. Ephesians 1 tells us that we have "every spiritual blessing" and outlines the blessings we enjoy as children of God.

- We are chosen in Christ.
- We are predestined for adoption.
- We have redemption through His blood.
- We have forgiveness of our sins.
- We have knowledge.
- We have an inheritance.
- We are marked with a seal.

In Christ we have everything we need to fight temptation and rise to challenges. While we will still struggle, Scripture promises us that sin will not have the final word, Christ will.

INTERNAL CHALLENGES

First, we'll turn our attention to internal challenges we might experience in regard to work. It's tempting to jump right into external challenges that many of us face, such as conflict with our coworkers or negotiating a raise, but the reality is that many of the fundamental challenges we face within our work are internal. There's always a temptation for work to creep into the extra crevices of our lives and become more preeminent than it ought to be.

Misplaced Mission

At the core of many of our challenges is a lack of remembrance of what our calling is when we work. We don't shed our call to be God's ambassadors when we step through the office doors or log into our computers. But so often, we forget throughout our days *how* our relationship with the Lord ought to shape us at work.

As Paul instructs us in Romans 12, we are, by the mercies of God, to "present your bodies as a living sacrifice, holy and acceptable to God, which is your spiritual worship. Do not be conformed to this world, but be transformed by the renewal of your mind, that by testing you may discern what is the will of God, what is good and acceptable and perfect" (vv. 1–2). Christ commands us to be transformed by the renewal of our minds, but I think many of us struggle to renew our minds when it comes to work. Our actions flow from what we believe to be true. For example, when we consistently overwork, we functionally behave as if that work is more important than our families, communities, church, or rest.

We might struggle with intense jealousy of others' positions because we believe that if someone else succeeds, we won't get promoted or able to secure a good job. Inwardly, we might wonder, *Will God really be good . . . to me?* So we covet and harbor envy in our hearts because of the success of others. Or we might scoff and just do the bare minimum because we don't like our boss or job, or we don't believe that our work really matters.

Personally, I struggle deeply with believing that I'm irreplaceable in my office, and I struggle setting and observing boundaries with my work. If I'm not careful, I can believe that my work is more important than it really is. I check emails constantly after work, even though there's no true emergencies, or work late to feel like I'm more dedicated than others.

We all have our own struggles and temptations with work. We also all need the Holy Spirit to renew our minds and transform every area of our lives. In cooperation with the Holy Spirit, we can identify areas of weakness that we individually struggle with and work on them. But on this side of eternity, our work will always be marred with struggle and sin.

While work is an important part of life, it is not ultimate.

People Pleasing

Almost every woman I know struggles in some way with pleasing people. The reality is, we all want to be liked by others. God created us to live and work in community, and people pleasing takes a good thing (living peaceably with others) and makes it supreme. Instead of our work being focused on serving others, we can get caught up in our ego. We'll wind up focusing more on *ourselves* and how *we* come across than on humbly serving others.

People pleasing can manifest itself in dozens of ways, but here are some examples:

- When asked for your opinion on a topic, you might not share honest feedback because you're afraid of how you'll be perceived.
- You might tell little white lies at work to look better. For example, when asked if you started a project, you might say that you have, even if you haven't.
- You might be tempted to behave at work in ways that are inconsistent with who you're called to be as a Christ follower.
- You join in office gossip because you want to fit in.

And the list could go on and on.

The solution to people pleasing is not to disregard what people think of us or to disparage ourselves. As Christians, we should be mindful of how our behaviors can impact others. Humility is the antidote to people pleasing. A. W. Tozer writes that "the victorious Christian neither exalts nor downgrades himself. His interests have shifted from self to Christ. What he is or is not no longer concerns him. He believes that he has been crucified with Christ and he is not willing either to praise or deprecate such a man."[2]

I personally spend time with the Lord in the morning, but by early afternoon, I'm usually caught up in the hurry of the day, the meetings, the deadlines, the weight of my work, and the problems I'm facing. If I'm honest, I often forget the truths I'd saturated my soul with just a few hours earlier. To help counter this forgetfulness, I've started carving out a few minutes midday to quiet my mind and spend a few moments in silent prayer. If I have time, I'll also try to read a psalm or another passage of Scripture. This small rhythm helps reorient my gaze back to the Lord and remind me of His purpose and vision for my life and work. Pausing to pray doesn't have to take much time, but the payoff has been extraordinary for me.

Building a new habit can be challenging, so I recommend setting an alarm on your phone to go off midday to remind you to cease laboring, even for a few small moments. Pray over the frustrating moments you've already experienced at work; pray for the coworker who's driving you nuts; pray for wisdom as you work, navigate a difficult conversation, or tackle a project that feels overwhelming. However people pleasing manifests in your life, I encourage you to build rhythms into your life that help you to regularly remember that we ultimately serve an audience of one.

Overworking

We live in a society where busyness is glorified. We cram our calendars with commitments—far too many of them—to make ourselves feel that our days have purpose and value. For many of us, our commitments do have deep significance and value. We're working extra hard on a time-sensitive project, volunteering to lead our child's field trip, and seeking to love our friends and families well.

I'm aware that some people don't have a choice but to work long hours. Perhaps you're a single mom trying to support your children, or perhaps you need to take on a side job to help make ends meet. There have been seasons of my life where I've needed to work extra hours to bring in additional income. Working longer hours out of necessity isn't the crux of what I'm addressing here. Many of us actually do have a choice for how we spend and steward our time, and we make the choice to overwork and to fill our calendars to overflowing.

By nature, I'm extremely driven and hardworking. I like to cross things off my to-do list and make progress on goals, dreams, and desires. I enjoy the satisfaction of a job well done. But it can be extremely tempting for me to allow work to have an outsized presence in my life. My mind is constantly telling me that I should be working quicker, harder, and longer. Those feelings are exaggerated when I hop on social media, and I'm met with posts telling me how hard others are seemingly working and all they've accomplished. The message I internalize is that, to measure up to others, I must not cease to work. So, I redouble my efforts to produce and prove myself and my worth.

How might this tendency toward overworking, comparison, and people pleasing show up in your own life? Maybe you recognize some of the following activities:

- You check in on email when you should be checking in on the hearts of your kids.
- You "like" a few photos on Instagram, when you should be giving verbal encouragement to your friends in real life.
- You don't establish boundaries with your phone and have it readily accessible at all hours.
- You use your phone in bed, leading to disruptive sleep patterns, which leads to persistent sleep deprivation.

This type of behavior is exhausting and demoralizing. But it is far too common. The glorification of busyness is related to the fact that our culture is one that's always connected. Technology is a wonderful gift;

with the touch of a button, you can call a friend, order groceries, share a picture of your new puppy, and so much more. But being constantly connected means that we can find ourselves tempted to always be working. Or at the very least, we can feel like we *should* be checking our notifications to make sure we didn't miss anything.

In order not to let work bleed over into every area of your life, we must embrace limitations. Oliver Burkeman, in his book *Four Thousand Weeks*, describes what a life lived with limitations looks like.

> A limit-embracing attitude to time means organizing your days with the understanding that you definitely won't have time for everything you want to do, or that other people want you to do—and so, at the very least, you can stop beating yourself up for failing.
>
> Since hard choices are unavoidable, what matters is learning to make them consciously, deciding what to focus on and what to neglect, rather than letting them get made by default—or deceiving yourself that, with enough hard work and the right time management tricks, you might not have to make them at all.
>
> It also means resisting the seductive temptation to "keep your options open"—which is really just another way of trying to feel in control—in favor of deliberately making big, daunting, irreversible commitments, which you can't know in advance will turn out for the best, but which reliably prove more fulfilling in the end.[3]

We can combat the endless cycle of overwork, exhaustion, and overcommitment by joyfully embracing limitations upon our life. I'm often reminded of the story of Mary, Martha, and Jesus in Luke 10. Scripture says that "Martha was distracted with much serving" (v. 40). She complains to Jesus and asks if He cares that Mary has left her to serve completely alone. Oh, how often I identify with Martha. I rush around serving, filling my moments with many good things, and wind up frustrated and exhausted. May Jesus' admonition pierce our hearts: "One thing is necessary. Mary has chosen the good portion, which will not be taken away from her" (v. 42).

The Lord formed us as finite beings, and we shouldn't try to do more than He has called us to do. In our work and our lives, may we focus on that which will not be taken from us.

Laziness

When we think of laziness, we often picture someone lounging around on the sofa, bingeing hours of Netflix, or goofing off at work. But laziness can often manifest in ways we might not immediately label as laziness. One of the biggest ways I've seen this play out in my own life is that I rest when I should be working and work when I should be resting. Let me give a more detailed example of what this looks like. When I'm at work, I'm often tempted to open my computer, check email, check Twitter, check Facebook, check Slack, and then finally start tackling my tasks. Fifteen minutes later, I'll go back through the entire process of checking everything again. If I'm not careful, I'll get sucked into not fully and deeply engaging in my work.

I often approach rest in a similar fashion. When I'm resting in the evenings or on the Sabbath, I'll spend hours on social media, responding to emails, or working on projects that don't require immediate attention. As a result, I'm not fully rested when I reengage with work. I sacrifice physical, emotional, and spiritual rest on the altar of squeezing in one more email. This type of behavior leads to a life that's never completely engaged in work or rest.

At its core, laziness is a mishandling of time. If we are indeed called to be stewards, we must give proper thought for how we spend our moments and how we spend our time. May we echo the prayer of the psalmist in Psalm 90:12: "So teach us to number our days that we may get a heart of wisdom." As we reorient our perspective on time, the late missionary Jim Elliot reminds us, "Wherever you are . . . be all there. Live to the hilt every situation you believe to be the will of God."[4] Each moment is a gift from the Lord, and we should be mindful that tomorrow isn't promised. May we work well and rest well.

Jealousy and Envy

The terms "envy" and "jealousy" are often used interchangeably but are actually distinct emotions. "Envy is a reaction to *lacking* something. Jealousy is a reaction to the *threat of losing* something."[5] I'll be honest, I struggle with both emotions more than I care to admit. Envy floods my heart when I see a woman obtain a professional achievement that I'm working toward, or I feel jealous when I feel that another colleague might threaten my role or my achievements.

Perhaps you've struggled with jealousy and envy too. It can be all too tempting to scroll through social media, get a quick peek at someone else's life, and feel envious because you don't have that thing, that accomplishment, or that type of relationship. In the workforce, struggling with envy and jealousy can often lead to competition with other women. We can feel like there's only so much room for women to be in leadership, so we must elbow others out on our way to the top. Or we might feel threatened when a new woman joins the staff and appears to be better at their job than we are at ours.

The reality is, there will always be someone smarter, prettier, more successful, or more on top of things. Competition with other women only harms us. We're eaten up inside with ugly feelings, rather than seeking to love, serve, and encourage others. As we battle jealousy and envy, we can use it as an opportunity to acknowledge the good gifts the Lord has given to someone else, reorient our hearts back to the Lord, and be content with what God has entrusted to us. As Linda Dillow writes, "Contentment is a state of the heart, not a state of affairs."[6] We can be content with what we have whether we're the CEO or the intern.

I've also greatly benefited from professional counseling (from a licensed professional counselor with a Christian worldview). Counseling has helped me in my personal and professional life, and I've explored some of my feelings and struggles that were laid out in this chapter. While I don't have the space to sufficiently explore all these challenges and ways to counter them, I recommend seeking out professional help if you're facing a particular intense struggle in one of these areas.

EXTERNAL CHALLENGES

Gossip

I've worked at both Christian organizations and secular workplaces, and one of the starkest differences is the amount of gossip that occurs within the secular workforce. That's not to say that it doesn't exist within a faith-based organization, but I've personally experienced much more overt gossip within non-faith-based workplaces. I confess that I've fallen prey to wanting to fit in with my coworkers and contributed to gossip. Afterward, I've always felt guilty because I know the words I said were unkind and hurtful. At its core, gossiping is disparaging another image bearer, and Christians have no business treating others in such a denigrating fashion. But the temptation to gossip can be strong for many of us. Personally, I've spoken in ways that I wish I hadn't, and close friends have shared with me that they also struggle with gossip too.

Gossip within secular places can often unify coworkers who otherwise might not have much in common. Complaining about your boss at lunch fills the conversation and colleagues can unite around a common "problem."

Gossip often takes on two forms. One is a mean-spirited critique of another person. This may look like tearing apart another person based on their appearance, personality, life decisions, workplace behavior, etc. I've overheard myself being gossiped about in this way. The coworkers gossiping about me didn't realize I'd walked into the room, and they were making fun of my appearance. Their taunting hurt me deeply.

The other form of gossip is complaining—complaining about a boss, a coworker, a project, or a decision that was made. While there's sometimes truth to this form of gossip—maybe your boss *is* difficult to work for or your coworker *did* dump a project on you last minute—gossip exacerbates the truth. Gossip doesn't do anything to solve the problem either; it just serves as an emotional release for the person doing the gossiping.

The book of Proverbs has much to say about how we use our words:

> "There is one whose rash words are like sword thrusts, but the tongue of the wise brings healing." (Prov. 12:18)
>
> "A soft answer turns away wrath, but a harsh word stirs up anger." (Prov. 15:1)
>
> "Gracious words are like a honeycomb, sweetness to the soul and health to the body." (Prov. 16:24)
>
> "Death and life are in the power of the tongue." (Prov. 18:21)
>
> "Whoever keeps his mouth and his tongue keeps himself out of trouble." (Prov. 21:23)

We should never forget how deeply powerful our words are. Even if the person we're gossiping about doesn't know, our behavior says something about our character. Christians are called to be set apart and holy, and we're also called to respect our fellow image bearers. If gossiping is a temptation for you, spend time before you begin work asking the Lord to help you fight the temptation to use your words in a harmful manner. Ask others to help keep you accountable as well.

Think about creative ways to steer a conversation away from gossiping and complaining. Ask someone about their weekend, their interests, their pets, their hobbies outside of work—really anything else to shift the conversation away from gossip. You could also come up with other ways to unify your colleagues. Perhaps you start a professional book club, or host monthly "lunch and learn" seminars. The key is to find other ways to connect with your colleagues instead of always defaulting to gossip.

Resolving Conflict

Inevitably, there will be disagreements and conflict within the workplace. Sometimes we sense that a coworker might be frustrated with us because they are being passive-aggressive. Other times, we don't have to wonder if someone is upset because they make it known to us . . . and to everyone else. Conflict within the workplace can result from poor communication, miscommunication, personality differences, workstyle differences, unmet expectations, or a lack of clarity.

Just as in a marriage or a friendship, people are going to accidentally step on one another's toes, fail to communicate well, or simply drop the ball. The goal of navigating conflict within the workplace isn't to avoid it altogether but rather to develop healthy ways for navigating conflict when it arises. Mutual respect and understanding go a long way. Don't immediately resort to being defensive but seek to understand why someone else is frustrated with you. It's best to have a one-on-one conversation with a coworker in a private location so you can talk honestly. If a conflict arises in front of others, try to table the conversation until you're able to cool down and have a rational conversation alone.

Hesha Abrams, a professional mediator, says that "most people have a point, even if you disagree with it. Don't dismiss them; try to see where they're coming from. Making people feel understood helps defuse the tension."[7] One practical way to do this is to ask clarifying questions about the situation. Try incorporating the phrase *I hear you* into your professional vocabulary. That simple phrase makes someone feel heard and understood.

Attempt to identify the actual problem you're trying to solve. This might sound simplistic, but oftentimes we can pile on the frustration when addressing an issue. For example, maybe someone dumped a time-sensitive project on your plate with unrealistic expectations for you. This might be a pattern of behavior, and you suddenly feel the need to address months' worth of frustration instead of addressing this isolated event. Focus on the problem at hand.

Lastly, try to always assume the best about people. As the saying goes: "Don't ascribe to malice what can be plainly explained by incompetence."[8] Someone might be weeks behind on a deadline, floundering around, and frustrating everyone in the process. Someone else might be learning on the fly, and truly not up to par on their job responsibilities yet, creating more work for others. Let's learn to be gentle with others.

I've navigated my fair share of conflicts within the workplace. While it's not pleasant in the moment, I'm always thankful afterward because all parties involved usually have had the opportunity to share their perspective, identify miscommunications and unmet expectations, apologize when necessary, and ultimately become stronger coworkers because of it.

Negotiating Salary and Raises

When I started off in my career, I had no clue how to negotiate my salary or ask for a raise. Many of the "soft" skills I needed for my professional life weren't taught in college or even in an internship program. Thankfully, one of my bosses helped coach me on best practices for approaching financial conversations within the workplace.

For many women, discussing money and finances is one of the most uncomfortable situations we find ourselves in. We think that if we simply work hard, our work will be noticed and properly financially rewarded. Or that a company will immediately offer us what we're worth in salary negotiations. But most of the time, that's not the case.

Negotiating Salary

When interviewing for a job and a prospective employer asks what you currently make, remember that you don't have to answer that question. When negotiating your salary with an organization, you're negotiating based on the job you've applied for, not based off what you currently make. If you're asked about your current salary, you can respond by sharing what your targeted salary range is.

> *Thank you for asking. Based on the job duties and requirements, and based on my experience, skill set, and what I'm bringing to the table, the range I'm looking for in this position is ____________.*

Next, always make a counteroffer. Most companies expect a prospective employee to make a counteroffer. Even if an organization counters your counteroffer, you'll likely be able to earn a little bit more than if you hadn't asked at all. It's important to remember that salary negotiation isn't personal at all; it's a part of the hiring process. And most of the time, you'll be working with the human resources department, not your prospective current boss. If these conversations are particularly difficult for you, ask a friend to help role play with you so you can practice confidently engaging in financial conversations.

Asking for a Raise

It's usually best to ask for a raise around the same time as your annual review. If your organization doesn't do annual reviews, you should ask for a yearly check-in conversation. Remember, you don't deserve a raise simply because you've been at an organization for a certain amount of time. When asking for a raise, you should demonstrate all the value you've added to the organization. In a conversation with your boss, come with tangible ways that you've met or exceeded expectations, how you've contributed to the success of the organization, and why you believe you've earned a raise.

> *Based off [XYZ] ways I've contributed to the company's success, I'd like to ask for a 5 percent raise [or—I'd like to ask for a raise of $5,000].*

CONCLUSION

While I feel like I've barely scratched the surface, I hope this has provided a helpful starting point for navigating some challenges that women face within the workforce. Let this be a starting point for you. Entire books have been written on each one of the topics I've addressed in this chapter, and I encourage you to keep reading and learning. In chapter 7, I'll be specifically addressing how to navigate gender and racial discrimination within the workplace. We'll unpack two of the largest challenges that females can face at work.

I've spent my entire career working in Washington, DC. If I'm honest, I'm often tempted toward cynicism or despair because I've seen and experienced the ugly underbelly of this city. I've watched leader after leader fail; I've watched good men and women misuse their power and influence. Good policies have failed, and bad ones have advanced. I've wept at the injustices I've observed and experienced. Like many of you, I've navigated challenges within the workplace, I've dropped the ball at work, and I've made mistakes. We can often feel like echoing the author of Ecclesiastes, "Vanity of vanities! All is vanity."

Steven Graber writes:

> There is much to be cynical about—and cynicism is a good answer if there has not been an incarnation. But if that has happened, *if* the Word did become flesh, and *if* there are

> men and women who in and through their own vocations imitate the vocation of God, then sometimes and in some places the world becomes something more like the way it ought to be.[9]

The good news of the gospel is that cynicism doesn't have the final word. Our challenges within our work can be redeemed because "He is making all things new."[10] God promises that nothing done for Him is ever in vain, even when met with difficulty. As we navigate challenging people and circumstances, may we extend the grace of God and rest in His peace and presence.

REFLECTION QUESTIONS

What are the specific internal and external struggles I face within my work?

How can I fight these temptations?

Who can I share my struggles with, and can they can help keep me accountable?

FURTHER READING

Respectable Sins—Jerry Bridges[11]

SCRIPTURE TO MEDITATE UPON

"Let all bitterness and wrath and anger and clamor and slander be put away from you, along with all malice. Be kind to one another, tenderhearted, forgiving one another, as God in Christ forgave you."

—Eph. 4:31–32

"Bearing with one another and, if one has a complaint against another, forgiving each other; as the Lord has forgiven you, so you also must forgive. And above all these put on love, which binds everything together in perfect harmony."

—*Col. 3:13–14*

Chapter 6

Leading with Confidence

How Women Can Lead, Mentor, and Serve Well Within Their Workplaces

The fact that I am a woman does not make me a different kind of Christian, but the fact that I am a Christian makes me a different kind of woman.

Elisabeth Elliot[1]

For hundreds of years, the leadership of women has impacted culture, society, and the spread of the gospel. Susan B. Anthony was a leader in the abolition of slavery and the right for women to own their own property and vote. Although totally blind, Fanny Crosby wrote over nine thousand hymns, many of which, like "Blessed Assurance," are still sung today. Charlotte "Lottie" Moon, one of the first single missionaries sent by Southern Baptists, served in China for over forty years. Amy Coney Barrett is a brilliant Supreme Court Justice, a mother of seven children, including several who joined their family through adoption, and a faithful, committed Christian.

While we know the lives and legacies of these women, there are countless other women whose names we'll never know but who have had a deep impact on the lives of others. While success isn't inherently bad or something to be avoided, we must never confuse success with faithful obedience to the Lord. If we climb the corporate ladder and make piles of cash but are dishonest or sacrifice our commitment to our family, community, and our church, we aren't successful in the eyes of the Lord.

Leadership is influence.[2] Each of us has the capacity to use our God-given gifts, skills, and passions to influence others, even if we don't have a title in front of our name. We might not think of ourselves as natural leaders, but we all possess the ability to influence others. Leadership is also stewardship. This is a common theme that keeps emerging in this book, but Christians interact with the world differently than nonbelievers. The world has seen far too many leaders who have wielded their power and influence for evil—Adolf Hitler, Benito Mussolini, and Kim Jong-un, to name a few, and each responsible for the deaths and oppression of millions of image bearers. Dictators are an extreme example. But sadly, leaders who put profits above people and work for selfish gain and ambition are far too common. Christians have a *responsibility* to steward our influence for the good of others and the glory of God.

Before we discuss some practical ways to strengthen our ability and capacity to lead, we must first discuss some characteristics of true leaders. John Mark Comer says that "what we *do* flows from who we *are*. Both matter."[3] We can't jump to action without first assessing our integrity.

FOCUS ON CHARACTER DEVELOPMENT

Leadership books are a dime a dozen. Many of them offer helpful principles and wisdom, and I've personally benefited from reading many of them. While working with excellence, sharpening your skills, and developing your gifts is an important part of developing your leadership, most fundamental is character development. People watch how we conduct ourselves, approach difficult situations, and how we speak to and about our colleagues. Our character shines through our words and deeds.

As my friend Ashley said, "The worst-case scenario is not the inability to use your gifts. The worst-case scenario is your gifts taking you to a place your character can't sustain you."[4] All of the women mentioned at the beginning of this chapter were able to do the work they did because of their faith and their strong character. When leadership is disconnected from strong character, ability alone cannot truly sustain you for the long haul. Our character, or lack thereof, usually comes out in difficult times.

Our perspective on leadership ought to be shaped by God's Word. Therefore, we should seek to develop the fruit of the Spirit—love, joy, peace, patience, kindness, goodness, faithfulness, gentleness, and self-control. And we should model ourselves after the example laid out in Psalm 1. May we delight in the law of the Lord, and seek Him, His strength, and His presence continually! As Proverbs 11:3 reminds us: "The integrity of the upright guides them." Let us commit to be people of excellent character and strong morals.

IMPOSTOR SYNDROME

I took a deep breath as I stepped into a meeting where I was presenting. I knew my material inside and out; I'd practiced and was well prepared. Yet, I was shaking in my stilettos, afraid that I didn't really belong in that room and that there was someone more qualified than I who deserved to be presenting. No one had told me that I shouldn't be there or scoffed at my remarks. What I was experiencing was something I think many women struggle with: impostor syndrome; the feeling that we don't belong, are undeserving of our achievements, aren't as competent or intelligent as others might think, and that one day people will discover who we really are—a *fraud*. Even Maya Angelou, the prizewinning author, struggled with impostor syndrome. She said after publishing her eleventh book that every time she wrote another book, she'd think, "Uh-oh, they're going to find out now. I've run a game on everybody."[5]

Women who struggle with impostor syndrome battle the nagging voice that they are not enough to tackle the challenges and opportunities set before them. Simultaneously, women have also been made to feel less than because of certain types of environments. Recently, at a girls night, we swapped stories of how we struggled with impostor syndrome. But we also shared how our male counterparts didn't appear to lack the confidence that we so desperately desired. Katty Kay and Claire Shipman, authors of *The Confidence Code*, accurately describe how many of us might feel:

> Women have long believed that if we just work harder and don't cause any bother, our natural talents will shine through and be rewarded. But then we have watched as the men around us get promoted over us and paid more, too. . . . When a man walks into a room, they're assumed to be competent until they prove otherwise. For women, it's the other way around.[6]

Some women adopt aggressive leadership styles, in an attempt to be taken seriously at work. We've seen stereotypes of these types of women portrayed in movies like *The Devil Wears Prada*. In trying to be strong leaders, they turn everyone off. Others swing to the opposite extreme, never speaking up in meetings, only offering opinions when asked, or constantly feeling too timid. Women who desire to sharpen their leadership skills might feel like they have to choose between ruthlessly exerting dominance or being demure and reserved. But the good news is, we don't have to go to extremes to be a successful leader.

FEMALE IN THE WORKPLACE

We don't have to check our femininity at the door of the workplace in order to be good leaders. We can step into the workforce, confident in who God made us as women. Men and women will lead differently, and the world needs both genders leading with excellence. Female leaders bring different skill sets, perspectives, and ideas to the table that, combined with their male counterparts', "help create innovative perspectives that lead to better decision-making as a whole for the business."[7]

Women have a unique impact on the world around us. For example, "peace agreements are 35% more likely to last at least 15 years if women leaders are engaged in its creation and execution," and "when women hold more executive leadership positions, their companies are 21% more likely to outperform the national average."[8] Rather than trying to compete with our male counterparts, may we lean fully into how God made us and use that to propel our leadership and our work.

While impostor syndrome is a challenge that many people face, the answer for Christians isn't to denigrate ourselves, but rather to shift the focus off ourselves. In *The Confidence Code*, the authors write that "confidence is linked to doing. Confidence is not letting your doubts consume you. It is a willingness to go out of your comfort zone and do hard things."[9] In order to fight this feeling that so many of us face, let's choose to confidently step into our God-given roles and assignments. Let us joyfully take active steps toward working hard and working well, for the good of others and the glory of God.

SERVANT LEADERSHIP

Jesus, in the gospel of Matthew, teaches His followers about true leadership. His teaching tells us what to prioritize.

> But Jesus called them to him and said, "You know that the rulers of the Gentiles lord it over them, and their great ones exercise authority over them. It shall not be so among you. But whoever would be great among you must be your servant, and whoever would be first among you must be your slave, even as the Son of Man came not to be served but to serve, and to give his life as a ransom for many."
> (Matt. 20:25–28)

Leadership isn't ultimately about you, but about those you're leading. In fact, some of the most influential and powerful people in the world have been servant leaders. The US military places an enormous emphasis on servant leadership. In an article for *Harvard Business Review*, the author writes that "military leadership is based on a concept of duty, service, and self-sacrifice."[10] Secular leaders are telling us what Christians already know to be true, and what our Savior modeled for us over two thousand years ago: "The last will be first, and the first last" (Matt. 20:16).

Founder of the modern servant leadership movement, Robert K. Greenleaf, says that "while traditional leadership generally involves the accumulation and exercise of power by one at the 'top of the pyramid' . . . the servant-leader shares power, puts the needs of others first and helps people develop and perform as highly as possible."[11] One of the ways we can practice servant leadership is by being intentional with our relationships.

If you're in charge of others, schedule time for one-on-one conversations where you can get to invest in that relationship. Trust rides on the rails of relationships.[12] Be interested in your colleagues as holistic people, not just coworkers. Give them space to bring up challenges they are facing, and regularly encourage them with what they are doing well and offer instructive feedback. If you don't have a leadership role within your organization, you can still intentionally build relationships with others. Consider identifying people you don't know well, reach out to them, and invite them to coffee or lunch.

The best leadership is born out of a commitment to serve.

Whether you're in a traditional leadership position or not, you can choose to honor your coworkers, customers, and work by developing a servant leadership posture. Some practical ways to develop a posture of servant leadership:

- Put people first
- Encourage employee participation
- Listen attentively without rushing to offer your own opinion or perspective
- Ask good questions
- Be willing to give and accept honest feedback
- Build trust with your employees by demonstrating that you have their best interest at heart
- Figure out what's impeding an employee's progress, and help them explore ways to overcome challenges

Work with Excellence

Our work says something about the God we serve. One of the ways we honor the Lord is by working with excellence. As Dorothy Sayers reminds us, "The only Christian work is good work well done. Let the Church see to it that the workers are Christian people and do their work well, as to God: then all the work will be Christian work, whether it is church embroidery, or sewage farming."[13] Paul writes in Colossians 3:23 that "whatever you do, work heartily, as for the Lord and not for men."

While I was working at the law firm, I resolved that I was going to be the best executive assistant I could possibly be. I showed up on time. I did my work thoroughly and well. I was kind and considerate of others. I built trust with my bosses and owned up to my mistakes quickly. As I built relationships with my coworkers, I was able to share my faith. On my last day at the firm, my boss told me that I was the best assistant he'd ever had. I was deeply grateful that my commitment to excellence had paid off, but more importantly, I was able to serve him well.

Whenever I feel distracted or unfocused, I also use those feelings as an opportunity to pray. I tell the Lord what I'm feeling—bored, unmotivated, stuck, or disenchanted—and I ask Him to help me navigate those feelings so that I can honor my employer and my work.

Whether you're stocking shelves at Walmart, teaching young minds, caring for sick bodies, or writing an email, remember that your work matters. God can be trusted in the seemingly small and insignificant, because His kingdom and economy look different from ours. Excellence not only says something about the character of God, but it simultaneously increases your value and potential in the workplace. We are reminded of this truth in Proverbs 22:29: "Do you see a man skillful in his work? He will stand before kings; he will not stand before obscure men." Be dependable. Honor your commitments. Under-promise and over-deliver. Treat everyone with dignity and value. Show up on time. Whether you're the CEO of a Fortune 500 company, or an intern at a small nonprofit, commit to doing everything with excellence.

SUPPORT OTHER WOMEN

In several of the places I've worked, my greatest struggles weren't difficult bosses, challenging workloads, or long hours, it was the other women I worked with. While there were some women I immediately bonded with, other relationships were much more difficult. I've felt ostracized and uncomfortable, as other women have made it clear how much they didn't like me.

Women can be one another's greatest threat and hurdle in the workforce. As a Christian woman in your workplace, seek to always be the first one to honor and uplift other women. Go out of your way to praise and recognize the work of other women. Send an encouraging email or text message. If you know one of your female coworkers is having an especially difficult season, offer to help take some tasks off her plate. We should be uplifting other women, not tearing them down.

Mentorship

When I first moved to Washington, DC, and started working full time, I made many professional faux pas, from how I dressed, to professionalism in the office. Thankfully, I had women in my life who taught me how to dress and act professionally. Sometimes, it was just a quick comment on ways I could improve. Other women took significant time to meet regularly with me and help me learn and grow. I still have a few women who I regularly reach out to whenever I have career questions, need help navigating a situation, need a safe place to chat about an issue, or just need some encouragement.

It's a professional priority of mine to pour into and mentor younger women. If an intern or a younger woman asks me to get coffee and chat, I do my absolute best to create time in my schedule. I was helped so much professionally when I was younger in my career, and as a result I have a strong desire to help others. Sometimes, I'll grab coffee with an intern a few times while they are in town for their internship program, and other times I've had more formalized mentorship relationships.

A powerful way each of us can lead professionally and support other women is to commit to mentoring younger women. Women intuitively understand some of the unique challenges that women face in the workforce and can help guide those a few steps behind them. When entering a more formalized mentor relationship, it's helpful to have clearly defined expectations. Some helpful questions to think through:

How long will you meet?
You might meet once a month for six months and then on a quarterly basis, as needed. Or you meet weekly for a month and then are available to schedule periodic phone calls moving forward. You might meet once or twice during someone's internship program.

How will you structure your time together?
Consider working through a set of questions your mentee has or reading and discussing a relevant book. You could also consider whether you'll spend the majority of your time on industry specific conversations, or if the topics you'll cover will be more general.

Will you meet one-on-one, or host small mentorship groups?
Both have their place and can be beneficial. For one-on-one mentorship, you're able to devote your focus and attention on one person, share individualized wisdom, and help them navigate specific circumstances. With group mentorship, women will be able to share and engage from different perspectives and backgrounds. Additionally, women will be able to build community with one another.

Your role as a mentor is to help sharpen, encourage, and edify younger women. One of the skills a successful mentor has is tactfully and humbly offering honest feedback. When I worked on Capitol Hill, I had to have several conversations with younger ladies about professional dress and behavior. While those conversations aren't pleasant, your feedback will hopefully help a younger woman more quickly develop professional behaviors.

It can be intimidating for younger women to reach out to those who are just a few steps ahead of them. Even in my thirties, I can still feel intimidated. It's tempting to believe that I'm bothering someone, using up too much of their time, or that they simply have better things to do. If I ask someone for coffee or to meet up, they have the option of saying no. But they cannot say yes if you don't ask.

If you have a desire to begin mentoring or pouring into younger women but don't know where to start, I suggest taking the initiative and offering. You can send out an email to the women on your staff. You can let your church or network know that you'd like to professionally mentor others. Developing younger women helps them to see what's possible and helps them not to make the same mistakes you once made. Model for other women what you wish had been modeled for you. Maybe you didn't have many examples of Christian leaders as you began your professional life, but you can choose to help develop the talents of other women and support them in a leadership pipeline.

Inner Circle

While it's important to regularly be pouring into younger women and helping others, it's equally important to have your own professional inner circle. Mine is very informal, but I have two or three trusted peers with whom I can navigate professional challenges and decisions. If I have a situation where I need some extra input, I'll give them a buzz and chat through the situation. If someone in your inner circle is in a similar profession or knows your organization well, you'll want to be careful that asking for advice doesn't turn into gossiping. You might have to be vague with some of the details in a particular situation. If you don't have an inner circle, I encourage you to write down the names of a few people who know you well and whose opinion and feedback you trust. Chances are, you will likely have at least one person in your professional life who would be a good fit. If not, prioritize developing relationships like this, so that you will have trusted professional colleagues who can pour into you.

Presentation Matters

How you present yourself matters and tells others that you take your job and work seriously. This doesn't mean that you need to go buy a whole new wardrobe or squeeze yourself into the world's standard of beauty. But it does mean that you should give some thought to presentation.

When I first moved to Washington, DC, the organization I worked for at the time had high expectations for what women ought to look like. The unwritten expectation often went above and beyond the organization's professional dress code policy. I barely made enough money to cover my rent, food, and transportation costs, much less purchasing new outfits. Even though I couldn't afford to get my nails done, buy new makeup, or keep up with the latest trends, I could come to work clean, fresh, and presentable.

Remember that confidence, kindness, and a smile go a long way.

AMBITION WITH WORK

Ambition, sadly, can get a bad reputation. Like anything else, ambition can be disproportionate in our lives. But an earnest desire for our work to have true and lasting impact isn't a wrong desire. As Dave Harvey writes in his book *Rescuing Ambition*: "We consciously pursue what we value. . . . We perceive something, prize it at a certain value, then pursue it according to that assigned value because we were created that way. This ability to perceive, prize, and pursue is part of our essential humanness, and it's the essence of ambition."[14] When we value our work, we will work hard with godly ambition. The work God has called us to is worth our appropriate dedication and value.

LEADERSHIP WITHIN THE COMMUNITY

In addition to leading within our professional workspaces, we can also lead within our communities. Vocation, after all, is much larger than our jobs. In her book *Kingdom Calling*, Amy Sherman says vocational stewardship is the "the intentional and strategic deployment of our vocational power—knowledge, platform, networks, position, influence, skills and reputation—to advance foretastes of God's kingdom."[15]

Scripture tells us that the Proverbs 31 woman "opens her hand to the poor" and "reaches out her hands to the needy."[16] She actively worked toward caring for the least of these within her community. We can leverage our work and vocational power both in our professional lives and outside of our nine-to-five. This is good news for those of us who might feel stuck or stagnant within our workplaces. Working for the good of our community is also a beneficial rhythm for those who are thriving in their professional lives. Serving is a reminder that the world is so much bigger than *our* world. When we intentionally choose to spend our time, talent, and treasure for the good of our neighbors, we are actively pointing the watching world to the character of God. Our lives are not our own, and we can joyfully endeavor to lead both within our workplaces and in our communities. May we lead and serve for the good of neighbor and the glory of God.

CONCLUSION

Our vocational service and commitment to others matters for today *and* eternity. Amy Sherman reminds us that "every faithful act of service, every honest labor to make the world a better place, which seemed to have been forever lost and forgotten in the rubble of history, will be seen on that day [at the final resurrection] to have contributed to the perfect fellowship of God's kingdom."[17] Every time we pour into others, work with excellence, steward our time, talent, and treasure, support other women, and confidently step into who God made us to be, we are reflecting our Creator God and using our gifts for His greater purpose.

REFLECTION QUESTIONS

How can you work with excellence?

Who in your life could you consider mentoring?

What are some practical next steps you can take after reading this chapter to strengthen your leadership?

FURTHER READING

The Confidence Cornerstone: A Woman's Guide to Fearless Leadership—Catherine Gates[18]

The Confidence Code: The Science and Art of Self-Assurance—What Women Should Know—Katty Kay and Claire Shipman[19]

Leaders Eat Last: Why Some Teams Pull Together and Others Don't—Simon Sinek[20]

SCRIPTURE TO MEDITATE UPON

"Iron sharpens iron, and one man sharpens another."

—*Prov. 27:17*

Chapter 7

Navigating Gender and Racial Discrimination

How to Stand Up for Yourself

Far from being antithetical to women's rights, Christianity is their firm and best foundation.

Rebecca McLaughlin[1]

Over coffee with girlfriends, I've heard story after story of sexism that women have faced within the workplace. Sometimes, the discrimination is overt and explicit and has left me speechless. Other times, it's more subtle, and we all roll our eyes and say, "That would never be said or done if it was a man." Other women I know have faced double discrimination of sexism and racism within the workplace. Far too many of us have been hurt by those who were supposed to protect us or to lead us well, without harming us.

I surveyed about seventy-five women for this book, and over half said that they'd experienced gender or racial discrimination.

MY OWN STORY WITH GENDER DISCRIMINATION

My boss on Capitol Hill resigned in the middle of his term during the #MeToo movement due to allegations of sexual misconduct. While I'm thankful that nothing inappropriate happened toward me, I had to pay the price of someone else misusing their power and authority in the workforce. I lost a job I loved and fielded prying questions from people. The initial allegations led to an inquiry into my boss's discussions with two female staffers about surrogacy. At the time, I was in the middle of writing *Longing for Motherhood*, in which I shared my personal story with childlessness and my inability to bear children. I'd publicly announced my book, and my boss and coworkers were aware of that part of my story. While I never would have written childlessness into my own story, I didn't know that it would be the thing that protected my reputation in this situation. Those who knew me and my story thankfully knew that no inappropriate conversations had taken place. But still, that didn't stop people who didn't know me well from trying to get the inside scoop and being extremely nosey about what happened.

I remember when the news broke on Twitter. I knew it was coming, but that didn't make it easier to read headline after headline about your office and field questions about the situation. As I grappled with losing my job in such a public fashion, I was also processing how to move forward after watching a man I'd so deeply respected publicly fail. During that season, I thankfully had close friends who walked through the hard days with me and gave me a safe space to process my anger, hurt, and frustration.

THE BIBLE AND SEXISM

Sexism and racial discrimination are an assault on human dignity and the *imago Dei* of every woman. God created men and women with *equal* dignity, worth, and value, and when someone is mistreated because of their sex or because of the color of their skin, they are ultimately insulting the Creator God who created women to uniquely reflect Him. As Christians, we must uphold the truth that all people are created in the image of God—both male and female. Nowhere in the Bible do we see that one sex is superior to the other. In Galatians,

Paul writes that "we are all one in Christ Jesus,"[2] meaning that what ultimately unites us isn't our sex, our ethnic background, or our role, but our sonship in Christ. Instead, we see our Savior upholding the dignity of women during His ministry on earth.

Throughout history, a woman's physical appearance has been valued as the most important thing about her. Beautiful women often turn the heads of men and receive more opportunities or attention. This devalues a woman and reduces her to nothing more than her physical or sexual appeal. Historian Tom Holland said that in Greco-Roman thinking, men were superior to women, and sex was a way to prove it. "As captured cities were to the swords of the legions, so the bodies of those used sexually were to the Roman man."[3] The conqueror branded the "conquered" inferior. Women in the ancient world had no control over their own bodies or their future. In ancient culture, they were vulnerable and mistreated. The prayers of Jewish men, in a patriarchal society, included a prayer of thanksgiving, "Praised be God that he has not created me a woman."[4]

Jesus' treatment of women was countercultural.

In one of the most remarkable stories in the Gospels, we see Jesus tenderly interact with the woman at the well. Not only was He speaking with a woman in public, He was speaking to a Samaritan. Cultural protocol dictated that Samaritans and Jews didn't interact, much less a Jewish man interacting with a Samaritan woman. Scripture doesn't name the woman, but it doesn't have to because Jesus did something more important. The Samaritan woman came to the well in the middle of the day when she thought no one would notice her drawing water. She was an outcast of society, shamed for her promiscuous behavior, yet in her conversation with Jesus, He treats her with kindness and interacts with her honestly. He doesn't shy away from addressing her sin but offers hope and healing.

As author Rebecca McLaughlin notes, "far from being antithetical to women's rights, Christianity is their firm and best foundation."[5] Throughout Jesus' ministry, He interacts with women, not based on their gender, but based on their common humanity.

MISTREATMENT OF WOMEN AROUND THE WORLD AND CLOSER TO HOME

When having a conversation about gender and racial discrimination, it's important to remember our sisters around the world who face oppression and persecution because of their gender. "Gendercide," the systematic killing of members of a specific gender, means many girls don't even have the chance at life. The United Nations estimates that approximately 140 million girls are missing from the world due to sex-selective abortions.[6] The UN says that increased sexual violence and trafficking have already been linked to gendercide. In North America, several thousand Indigenous women have been murdered or gone missing "because of their gender."[7] In addition to the millions of females missing around the world, women and girls are routinely abused and mistreated physically, emotionally, and sexually.

A few years ago, I attended the State Department's Ministerial to Advance International Religious Freedom and heard Nobel Peace Prize winner Nadia Murad share her story.[8] Murad recounted her harrowing story of capture and sexual slavery by ISIS leaders. Nadia was a member of the Yazidi community and was born in northern Iraq, where she happily spent her days with her family and tight-knit community. When ISIS attacked Nadia's village, they separated the women and girls from the men, and most of the women were held hostage as sex slaves. A high-ranking ISIS official purchased Nadia, and she was subjected to repeated sexual abuse and rape.

In her autobiography, Nadia tells of her first attempted escape and how, when her captor found out, he allowed her to be gang raped by his subordinates. Then, he promptly sold her to another ISIS leader. Eventually, she was able to bravely escape with the help of local villagers. Since then, she courageously speaks out about sexual violence being used during war. During her Nobel Lecture, she highlighted the plight that millions face around the world:

> Every day I hear tragic stories. Hundreds of thousands and even millions of children and women around the world are suffering from persecution and violence. . . . Every day we see hundreds of women and children in Africa and other countries becoming murder projects fuel for wars, without anyone moving in to help them or hold to account those who commit these crimes.[9]

Even in places where women should be most loved and protected, such as the church, they have experienced mistreatment and discrimination. Allegations have been made against long-standing and well-respected church and ministry leaders, evidence that no part of society is unscathed from the evils of sexual abuse or mistreatment of women.

While men and women are created with equality, dignity, worth, and value, sadly, society does not often value men and women equally. Whether it's in remote villages in the Middle East, at the hands of abortionists snuffing out the lives of baby girls, or churches and workplaces in the West, far too many women have faced oppression and violence simply because they are women.

Discrimination in the Workplace

The #MeToo movement was started when women who'd experienced rape, sexual abuse, or sexual harassment started speaking out. Massive industries like Hollywood, the media, professional sports, and politics were all implicated in scandal. However, women have experienced more micro-level discriminations within their workplaces, such as ageism and being discriminated against because they appear to be too old or young for certain roles, being overlooked for promotions simply because they are women, making less than their male counterparts, and having comments made about their physical appearance.

Below, I share stories of a few women I surveyed about what they experienced in the workforce. Some of these stories touch more on male/female dynamics within the workplace, and others touch on harassment. Names have been changed to protect privacy.

> Sarah:
>
> I'm older so I have experienced sexism in many instances. I had an interviewer ask me on a date during an interview. I had a boss comment on my body and always trying to touch me during work time. (I quit.) I didn't experience this hardly at all when I [first] became a teacher. I think the laws now help a lot. I worked with a few men in administration who would speak down to women in the workplace. They have called true concerns "mama drama." Many times their unwillingness to listen to females has cost them dearly down the road. Two women at my Christian workplace had to have their husbands come meet with the administration before their concerns were heard. The men received a different posture from the administration. Only then did the administration act.
>
> Jackie:
>
> Boys' clubs are real and difficult to navigate. Even when all the men in the group are generally thoughtful people, there's a lot of work that happens when they all go out for coffee and don't invite me. It sometimes means I miss out on conversations that would help me do my job better. I've worked with

men who did not take women seriously and doubted their ideas more than they would those of other men. I do not have a good solution for dealing with this! I've found it helpful getting support from other women—going with another person, maybe someone more senior, can be useful. I've also worked with men who would look me up and down when I arrived at work—it's an incredibly uncomfortable experience. I was pretty new to the workforce when this was happening and didn't know how to deal with it or raise it with anyone.

Challenges Women of Color Face in the Workforce

According to the law, race discrimination involves

> treating someone (an applicant or employee) unfavorably because he/she is of a certain race or because of personal characteristics associated with race (such as hair texture, skin color, or certain facial features). Color discrimination involves treating someone unfavorably because of skin color complexion. Race/color discrimination also can involve treating someone unfavorably because the person is married to (or associated with) a person of a certain race or color.[10]

One woman I surveyed shared with me that she once applied for a job that she was more than qualified for but wasn't hired. But she noticed that all the young women working there were of the same race—a race that she was not. She said that the interview only lasted about twenty minutes, and the manager did not seem very interested in interviewing her when he saw her.

Another woman shared that she worked on an entirely white staff. She is married to a Hispanic man and constantly experienced racist comments said about him and other Hispanic people. She said that she learned to be brave and push back against the comments her coworkers were making. She also reported behavior to her supervisors and corporate, causing them to implement training on the matter.

Several women shared frustration over how little their voices (black female voices) were heard, compared to the voices of their male counterparts. Others shared that they felt like they'd been hired in part because of the color of their skin, but their perspectives weren't taken seriously once they were on staff.

One area that women of color face is raced-based hair discrimination. The Legal Defense Fund says that "policies that prohibit natural hairstyles, like afros, braids, Bantu knots, and locs, have been used to justify the removal of Black children from classrooms, and Black adults from their employment."[11] A recent study by Michigan State University found that "black women with natural hair are often seen as less professional and less competent."[12] Research also determined that "80 percent of African American women felt they needed to switch their hairstyle to align with more conservative standards in order to fit in at work."[13] While bipartisan legislation has been introduced to address this issue, it hasn't been passed or signed into law yet. Companies have the ability to create dress code and grooming policies, but discriminating against natural hair goes well beyond the boundaries of a professional dress code.

WHAT TO DO IF FACED WITH DISCRIMINATION

If you've faced sexual harassment or discrimination at work, let me be the first to say that I'm so sorry that happened to you. What happened is wrong, and you shouldn't have been sinned against in that way.

If you were raped or sexually abused in the workforce, go to the police immediately. Both are criminal offenses. Racial discrimination and sexual harassment are against the law. If you've experienced either of these, file a formal complaint with HR. This should trigger an official investigation. It's also important to tell trusted people in your life.

Going to your supervisor or to HR can feel very intimidating because you're sharing difficult information with them. Consider having someone else come with you, so you're not alone. Navigating these situations can be difficult and emotionally taxing, so it can be helpful to put strong support systems in place. Find a trusted counselor who can help you process your circumstance. Share with trusted people in your life who can pray with and for you and encourage you spiritually.

Sadly, filing a complaint with HR doesn't mean that the issue will be properly handled. One woman I spoke with said that she tried to speak out but was threatened with being fired if she did. If something like this happens, you can file a complaint with the Equal Employment Opportunity Commission (EEOC). You are protected from retaliation if you file a charge of discrimination with the EEOC. Several women I surveyed disclosed that they ended up leaving jobs because of sexual harassment. If your situation isn't properly dealt with by your company's human resources department, I encourage you to begin looking for other jobs. While it's wrong that *you* must be the one to leave, it's better than staying in a situation where your supervisors or HR department won't protect you.

SPEAK UP FOR WOMEN

Our faith should compel us to speak up on behalf of persecuted and vulnerable people. In fact, one of the lessons that King Lemuel's mother taught him in Proverbs 31 was the importance of being a voice for the voiceless: "Open your mouth for the mute, for the rights of all who are destitute. Open your mouth, judge righteously, defend the rights of the poor and needy" (Prov. 31:8–9).

Women are not second-class to men; rather they are intrinsically valuable and worthy to God. God cares deeply about women, and so must we. Whenever we see women being mistreated because of their gender, race, or age, we should be the very first ones to condemn such wicked behavior and stand up for those who are facing discrimination.

CONCLUSION

This was the hardest chapter to write. As I typed out the words, I saw the faces of my friends who've been mistreated because of their age, gender, or skin color. I've also been reminded of the stories of women around the world and throughout history who've experienced gross violations of their dignity and worth. Men and women were created to be co-heirs with the Lord, but in a world marred by the fall, women are often the ones who pay a heavier price.

Dear reader, I don't know what you've experienced in your life. If sexual abuse or racial discrimination is a part of your story, please know that I've prayed over these words, and I've prayed for you. I hope that your heart is comforted by our Savior, who always treated women well. If you haven't experienced mistreatment in the workforce, would you pause and pray for your sisters who have? And would you use your voice to advocate for others who are mistreated? We can be a part of the solution when we resolve not to remain silent when others are being mistreated.

God promises to be near to the brokenhearted. May you feel His tender love and care for you.

REFLECTION QUESTIONS

Have you personally experienced sexism and/or racism in the workplace?

If so, how have you navigated it?

If not, have you seen others being mistreated in the workplace because of their gender, age, or race?

What are some active ways you can use your voice to advocate for other women?

FURTHER READING

Jesus through the Eyes of Women: How the First Female Disciples Help Us Know and Love the Lord—Rebecca McLaughlin[14]

SCRIPTURE TO MEDITATE UPON

"There is neither Jew nor Greek, there is neither slave nor free, there is no male and female, for you are all one in Christ Jesus."

—*Gal. 3:28*

Chapter 8

The Secret to Flourishing

Why Sabbath and Rest Are Vital

The result of busyness is that an individual is very seldom permitted to form a heart.

Søren Kierkegaard[1]

My lowest point in recent memory was on an American Airlines flight, headed to visit family. As soon as the pilot gave the green light, I reached into my backpack for my laptop, settling in to work on the three-hour flight. But there was a hiccup in my plan; my computer wouldn't turn on. Nothing I tried worked, foiling my goal of cleaning out my inboxes and catching up on some projects. Instead of accepting reality and pulling out a book, I had a complete meltdown. I sat in seat 27C and sobbed till my eyes were red. My computer not turning on shouldn't have been a big deal, but it was. This incident occurred after I'd been to the Apple store three times within a few days, struggling to resolve computer issues. My latest computer woe was literally the straw that broke me. This incident occurred at the end of 2020, a year that left most of us weary and emotional.

Perhaps you can relate. Working during "normal times" might have felt challenging enough, but navigating working (or looking for a new job) during a global pandemic might have caused you to feel like you're drowning. On top of that, many of us were homeschooling children, or battling loneliness, anxiety, financial pressures, and family dynamics. As the world has returned to a new normal, fatigue still characterizes our soul. Our weekends are often filled with activities and chores, as we prepare to head back into another work week. We might grab the latest productivity book that promises to teach us new tips and tricks for getting more done, faster, and better. Or we might just try to work harder and harder, to try to finally "catch up" and get it all done.

For weeks leading up to the mile high meltdown, I'd been deeply struggling with exhaustion and anxiety. As I entered the end of the year, it felt as if the dam broke and the floodwaters of everything in 2020 rushed over me. I spent weeks and weeks slogging through each day, downing one cup of coffee after another, trying to find energy to complete my work. On top of my work, my husband and I were pursuing international adoption and had mountains of paperwork to complete in the evenings. Many days at the end of 2020 felt like a fight—to keep trusting the Lord's promises and to live faithfully in the season the Lord has placed me in.

Something had to change. I wasn't in a healthy place, and I didn't want to keep just barely getting by, hoping I had the energy to make it to bedtime. Pre-pandemic, I'd been fairly disciplined about boundaries with my phone, observing a day of rest, and filling my days and weeks with activities that helped me thrive holistically. But the pandemic turned my life upside down, and I was forced to relearn new rhythms. Many of us might be at the end of ourselves and know that something needs to change. We all want healthy souls, and thankfully, Scripture teaches us how to tend well to them.

THE ANSWER TO OUR STRIVING

The answer to our striving isn't to hustle harder, take a longer nap, or clear the decks. Rather, our souls desperately need to find their rest in the Lord. In the Psalms, we are reminded of God's character. He is our rock, our hiding place, and the restorer of our souls. He gives

His beloved sleep. And He has promised to be our shepherd, to lead us beside still waters and that in His presence we have no lack. He will never leave or forsake His children, no matter how exhausted we feel. Oh, how desperately our souls regularly need to be reminded of these glorious promises.

> "In peace I will both lie down and sleep; for you alone, O Lord, make me dwell in safety." (Ps. 4:8)
>
> "The Lord is my shepherd; I shall not want. He makes me lie down in green pastures. He leads me beside still waters. He restores my soul. He leads me in paths of righteousness for his name's sake." (Ps. 23:1–3)
>
> "For God alone my soul waits in silence; from him comes my salvation. He alone is my rock and my salvation, my fortress; I shall not be greatly shaken." (Ps. 62:1–2)
>
> "It is in vain that you rise up early and go late to rest, eating the bread of anxious toil; for he gives to his beloved sleep." (Ps. 127:2)
>
> "I wait for the Lord, my soul waits, and in his word I hope; my soul waits for the Lord more than watchmen for the morning." (Ps. 130:5–6)

We were created to find our rest in God alone, and our work is meant to flow out of that rest. In St. Augustine's *Confessions*, he reminds us that "God has made us for Himself, and our heart is restless until it rests in Him."[2] Only when we understand that our hearts will find true rest in the heart of God will we ever be able to live and work freely. Many of us are quick to blame technology and our fast-paced lives as the reasons for our weariness. But throughout human history, people have been struggling with restlessness and weariness apart from the Lord. May we lean into His character.

Jesus Secured Our True Rest

God is the giver of true rest, and we have access to it through Jesus' actions on our behalf at Calvary. In John 15:4–5, as Jesus is preparing for the cross, He says that the secret to bearing fruit is to abide in Him. He earnestly reminds us that apart from Him, we can do *nothing.* The abiding, the dwelling, and the resting is where we remember the truth about ourselves and the world. Yet, many of us still struggle. Amid our strife, Jesus extends a life-changing invitation to us.

> "Come to me, all who labor and are heavy laden, and I will give you rest. Take my yoke upon you, and learn from me, for I am gentle and lowly in heart, and you will find rest for your souls. For my yoke is easy, and my burden is light." (Matt. 11:28–30)

Dane Ortlund, in his wonderful book on this passage of Scripture, offers these insightful comments on Jesus' call to come to Him.

> You don't need to unburden or collect yourself and then come to Jesus. Your very burden is what qualifies you to come. No payment is required; he says, "I will give you rest." His rest is gift, not transaction. Whether you are actively working hard to crowbar your life into smoothness ("labor") or passively finding yourself weighed down by something outside your control ("heavy laden"), Jesus Christ's desire that you find rest, that you come in out of the storm, outstrips even your own.[3]

Resting from our work and abiding is not only an act of obedience to Christ, but it serves as a gospel reminder for us. If we can trust Him for our salvation and redemption, we can trust Him with the details of our lives. We don't have to earn God's rest; He's already given it to us.

- The gospel reminds us that no amount of work can earn what we ultimately need—forgiveness and redemption for our sins.
- The gospel reminds us that we can cease our striving, because there's nothing we can ultimately do to earn God's favor or love.
- The gospel reminds us that the fruit we bear must come from a place of abiding in Jesus.

We should regularly fix our gaze upon the cross—there we are reminded of God's promises and provision. He promises to finish the work He began in us, and that is indeed good news for our weary souls.

THE CALL TO REST

Even with this glorious gospel reality, many of us still struggle to rest. When we fail to structure our lives within the boundaries the Lord has set for us, we're believing the lie that the serpent whispered into Eve's ear in the garden: "Did God really say . . . ?" Here are some of the ways that temptation might arise in your heart:

> "Does God really expect me to rest? Doesn't He know how many balls I'm juggling right now?"
>
> "Doesn't God know how important this big project is? I'll rest when it's over."
>
> "I'll prioritize rest once life slows down; once I cross this item off my to-do list; once the holidays are over; once the kids are older."
>
> "The Christian leader I respect doesn't seem to rest, and they seem to be very successful. Why do I need to rest?"

The reality is we all need respite. Yet so many of us behave as if we're superhuman and we try to defy our innate need for rest. God is limitless. We are not. Our need for rest serves as a regular reminder of our limits and frailty. When we grow tired, our weariness reminds us that our bodies and souls weren't created to work or produce all the time. We are humans, not machines. When we rest, we acknowledge our neediness. If we're honest with ourselves, we don't often like admitting that we need help. We want to be self-sufficient, and often bristle at any reminders that we're not. Pridefully, we might try to optimize our moments and days so that we squeeze every ounce of productivity out. And if we don't, we beat ourselves up for not trying harder.

Many of us often tell ourselves and our families that once we meet the next deadline or complete the next project, then we'll be able to engage with our full presence, and we'll stop to rest. But the goalposts always seem to be moving. The world tells us that we need to be slimmer, join the 5:00 a.m. club, write the next bestseller, have a perfectly organized home, succeed at work; all without dropping the ball in other areas of life. Social media tells us all the things that we could do, wear, places to go, things to own, and things we're missing out on. Stores allow us to utilize tools like "buy now, pay later" that give us what we want in the moment, and allow us to pay for the consequences later. We are also told that our identity is in our achievements.

But Scripture has a better story to tell:

- The Word invites us to cast our burdens upon the Lord, and He will sustain us. (Ps. 55:22)
- The Word reminds us that we are kept in perfect peace, when our mind is stayed on Him. (Isa. 26:3)
- The Word reminds us that the Lord daily bears us up. (Ps. 68:19)

Rest forces us to accept our limitations. As Kelly Kapic writes in *You're Only Human*, "Finitude is an unavoidable aspect of our creaturely existence." He explains that denying it could cripple us in unexpected ways, and even distort how we view God and "what Christian spirituality should look like."[4] God created us with limits, and they teach us dependence upon the Lord. Our limits are a good thing, not only because they are a gift from God, but they help us slow down and rightly order our lives and our loves.

Charles Spurgeon, known as the "Prince of Preachers," was prolific during his lifetime. Today, there is more available material written by Spurgeon than by any other Christian author, living or dead.[5] Yet, he deeply understood the value of rest and taught that "rest time is not waste time. It is economy to gather fresh strength. It is wisdom to take occasional furlough. In the long run, we shall do more by sometimes doing less."[6] Rest is how we sustain our work for the long term. Our lives must be structured in such a way that we can run the race with endurance. We don't work *for* rest, but *from* rest.

When we rest, we are acknowledging that the burdens of this world don't rest on our shoulders, they rest on His. His shoulders are strong enough to bear up the load. The Lord's call on our lives is faithfulness, and we can leave the results of our work in His hands. As we rest, we're demonstrating to the watching world the goodness of God. He created humans to flourish holistically and orchestrated rhythms of rest for our good. Rest is an act of dependence upon God; it is an act of trust.

Different seasons of life mean that rest will look different. You might have a newborn baby and rest feels like a distant memory, or you might be facing a particularly challenging circumstance that demands more of you. In difficult seasons, our need for rest becomes even more important because those circumstances are pulling and stretching us. In those scenarios, we might have to pull back in other areas of life to ensure we're still carving out the time to rest.

Rhythms of Sabbath

Sabbath is a regular rhythm we practice to rightly order our lives. It is how we practically live a life of rest. The word "sabbath" comes from the Hebrew word *Shabbat*, which means "He rested."[7] Shabbat originated from the beginning of Genesis when the Lord rested on the seventh day. However, the first mention of "sabbath" is in Exodus 16. God led the Israelites out of slavery from Egypt. As God's chosen people adjusted to a new way of life, the Lord promised to sustain them with His presence and by meeting their daily needs. He provided daily bread. Each morning, the Israelites were to gather enough food for the day. Worms and a foul smell appeared in the bread of those who disobeyed and hoarded more than they needed. The Israelites who gathered excess were demonstrating a lack of trust in God's promise to provide. On the sixth day, the Lord commanded the Israelites to gather twice as much bread in preparation for the Sabbath. Disobedient Israelites were left without food the next day. Throughout the Old Testament, God gave the Israelites governing laws for their Sabbath practices. In Egypt, the Israelites were slaves, "machines in the national economy."[8] Under slavery, they had no autonomy over their time, but were instead "victims to the inhumane logic of productivity."[9] But when God called His people out of Egypt, He instituted Sabbath as a way to teach them how to be fully human and rest in Him. As Jen Pollock Michel writes, "They were instead freed to flourish in ways unimagined. They were freed to be still and know that God was God. They were freed to resist, even to rest."[10] These rhythms of Sabbath were meant to teach the people of God how to ultimately rely on Him and His provision.

Jesus came to fulfill the law, and Scripture tells us that "the Sabbath was made for man, not man for the Sabbath. So the Son of Man is lord even of the Sabbath" (Mark 2:27–28). In these verses, Jesus proclaimed that He is the one who has authority over all things, including the rules that previously governed Sabbath practices.

Just as the Lord promised to provide for the Israelites, He promises to care for His children today.

We are made in God's image. God rested and so should we. In Genesis, after God was finished creating the world, He "blessed the seventh day and made it holy . . . [and] rested from all his work" (Gen. 2:3). This rhythm of rest was a part of God's original design, before sin entered the world. The word "holy" means to be set apart. Sabbath is meant to be a gift for the children of God; a time where we step back from ordinary life, delight in God's good gifts, and rest. The purpose of Sabbath is setting aside a day and reorienting our lives back to the Lord. Because God modeled rest for us, we should structure our lives in such a way that we regularly incorporate Sabbath rest.

Why We Honor Sabbath

Many people choose to observe Sabbath on Sunday, but for some, that's not the best option. Pastors and their families often observe their Sabbath on another day since their Sundays are often filled with work. If you work in a job with unpredictable hours, you might have to adjust the day you observe Sabbath. If you're new to this practice, I'd suggest choosing a day of the week where you can mostly take the day off. Not everyone has the ability to take an entire day off—that's okay. We are no longer bound by the law and don't have to abide by the strict Sabbath rules.

Observing a regular Sabbath is devoting a seventh of our lives to rest, and that might feel impossible for us. For those who constantly feel behind and are scrambling just to keep the house clean, the kids fed, and get to work on time, stepping away for any period of time might feel unrealistic. We can barely stay on top of things as it is—how on earth will we keep up if we observe Sabbath?

The reality is, we'll never "get it all done." There will always be more laundry to do, another email to answer, another area of your house to tidy, or something else you could be doing. Many of us subconsciously know that we'll never live up to the standard of perfection we've set for ourselves, but we hustle after it anyway. Many times, we've decided that everything must be done—*perfectly*. But that's completely unrealistic. We often confuse what *must* be done with what we'd *like* to get done. We need to accept our limitations, our capacities, and entrust the undone things to the Lord. We need to train ourselves to rest amid the undone.

God's economy is different from ours. In God's economy, there's more than enough. We don't have to compete with ourselves or others to receive God's promises, love, or acceptance. We already have it.

In the Sermon on the Mount in Matthew 5–7, just a few verses after Jesus reminds us not to lay up treasures for ourselves on earth, He reminds us of God's great care for His children. Many of us understand that our heart lies with our treasure, but still struggle to navigate the harsh realities of life. Jesus has an answer for our weary hearts: lift our gaze.

> "Your heavenly Father knows that you need them all. But seek first the kingdom of God and his righteousness, and all these things will be added to you. Therefore do not be anxious about tomorrow, for tomorrow will be anxious for itself. Sufficient for the day is its own trouble." (Matt. 6:32–34)

The Lord already knows what we need and promises to provide for His children. Sabbath is a time for us to remember that the Lord is ultimately the one who preserves us, provides for us, protects us, and loves us. Regularly observing a Sabbath is a way to uproot idols from our heart. How quickly other idols seem to creep into our lives, and for many of us, we're tempted to make an idol out of work. Sabbath reminds us to rightly order our lives and root out idols we've been relying on.

Observing Sabbath

Observing Sabbath will look different throughout the seasons of life. Sabbath for a single woman will be structured differently than it will for women with young children or those caring for an aging parent. As you begin to observe Sabbath, it's important to note your season of life and structure your Sabbath accordingly. One of the beauties of rest is that there's no prescription for what it ought to look like. Because we're all uniquely created with different personalities, needs, desires, and capacities, intentional rest will look different for each one of us. The goal isn't comparing and coveting what you wish you had or what rest looks like for others. It is to figure out how *you* can rest in the season entrusted to you.

When we regularly observe Sabbath, we *will* have to sacrifice in some way. As Walter Brueggemann said, "People who keep sabbath live all seven days differently."[11] Perhaps that sacrifice is extra work the day before your Sabbath, to lighten your burden on Sabbath. This could look like cleaning the house the day before so you can rest and don't feel pressured to clean. Or cooking an easy meal to heat up, so you don't have to spend hours in the kitchen. To rest for an extended period, many of us need to prepare ahead of time. Perhaps the sacrifice might feel more costly. You might have a coworker who works weekends to get ahead, and you feel pressure to work weekends as well to prove that you're a committed employee. Sabbath is countercultural, and it is always worth the price we pay. As Christians, we understand that the structure and priorities of our lives will be different from our peers who don't know the Lord. As you step deeper into this ancient practice, be gentle with yourself. You don't have to figure it all out at once. It'll likely take some trial and error as you practice, but we get fifty-two opportunities to strengthen that muscle throughout the year.

Worship

Set aside extended time to be alone with the Lord on Sabbath. Because many of us choose Sunday to observe Sabbath, trying to squeeze this time in before church might not be the best for you. Because the goal of Sabbath is reorienting our lives back to God, I encourage you to find time throughout the day to spend delighting in the Lord. Perhaps this looks like meditating upon your favorite psalm, spending extended time in prayer, or taking time praising the Lord for His good gifts in your life. Eugene Peterson reminds us that "Sabbath [is] uncluttered time and space to distance ourselves from the frenzy of our own activities so we can see what God has been doing and is doing."[12]

Delight

James 1:17 tells us that "every good gift and every perfect gift is from above, coming down from the Father of lights." All that's good in the world is from the Lord. We ought to take deep delight in the gifts the Lord has created for us for our enjoyment.

Dan Allender wrote that,

> The Sabbath is an invitation to enter delight. The Sabbath, when experienced as God intended, is the best day of our lives. Without question or thought, it is the best day of the week. It is the day we anticipate on Wednesday, Thursday and Friday—and the day we remember on Sunday, Monday, and Tuesday. Sabbath is the holy time where we feast, play, dance, have sex, sing, pray, laugh, tell stories, read, paint, walk, and watch creation in its fullness.[13]

Humans are holistic creatures, and we should structure our Sabbath with activities to refresh and rejuvenate both the body and soul. For me, these activities include going for a long walk outside without headphones, giving my soul space to breathe, deep conversation with a close friend, reading good fiction, and taking a hot bath. Take out a sheet of paper and jot down the activities you and your family enjoy. Perhaps you love to cook but are often rushed throughout the week; set aside time on Sabbath to cook a fun new recipe or bake a delicious treat. Perhaps you enjoy painting, but it's not high on your to-do list throughout the week. Gather your supplies and paint away on Sabbath. God gave us good gifts—may we delight in them.

Sabbath with Others

One of the joys of Sabbath is extended time to enter into relationships with others, linger over deep conversations, and spend time in community. Throughout the Bible, Christians are commanded to be a communal people. We weren't created to walk through life alone. God has called His church to enter into community with other believers. This is one of the ways we practically care for our brothers and sisters in Christ. But to live in community, we must set aside time to get to know one another and be known by others. Trust and depth of relationship are built over time, with an investment of time and commitment. Consider setting aside a portion of your Sabbath to spend in community with others. Perhaps you and your family always invite someone to have lunch with you on your Sabbath, or you go for walks with a friend in the afternoon. Celebrating the Sabbath with others is an excellent way to refresh our souls and bear the burdens of our community.

Digital Sabbath

Each of us likely spends more time on our phones and with technology than we'd care to admit. Apple always sends me my screen time report on Sunday morning, and I'm met with a weekly tinge of guilt over spending more time on technology than I meant to that week. Another vital part of a regular rhythm of rest ought to be resting from technology. By stepping away from social media and our phones for a period, we begin to loosen the grip technology has on so many of us.

For many of us, it's impractical to turn off our phones for twenty-four hours because we need to be available for emergencies. The good news is we don't have to completely shut off our phones to still rest from technology. The iPhone has settings where you put your phone on "do not disturb" but still allow for certain people to call or text. I have different settings for different times throughout the week. I have a "work focus mode," where I'm alerted of notifications from my husband and my coworkers. Catching up on the group texts can wait, but that way, I'm not missing anything important. I also have a "personal focus mode" that I turn on in the evenings and on the weekends. You could also consider deleting social media apps from your phone during your Sabbath.

As you can probably tell from my opening story, I wasn't in a good place at the end of 2020. I was regularly falling asleep to TV, scrolling social media for far too long, and I would immediately check my phone when I woke up. These behaviors were unhealthy for me; I was turning to my phone as a place of rest and refuge, instead of giving my soul space. Perhaps you can relate. By incorporating a digital Sabbath, we slowly retrain ourselves not to immediately turn to technology to soothe our tensions or give us a quick hit of dopamine when we're feeling down or bored. Stepping away for a period of time helps us slow down and begin turning to the Lord in the moments when we're normally reaching for our phones.

I admit that I observe this practice imperfectly, but I know how important it is for my soul, and I strive to incorporate it into my weekly Sabbath. One of the most impactful rhythms I started practicing a few years ago was taking the month of August entirely off social media. Personally, this month works well for me. Congress is in recess during the entire month of August, which means my work is quieter, and I'm able to slip away with relative ease. I know people who begin a new year by taking January off social media to hit "reset." As you think through what boundaries with technology and social media look like for you and your family, I'd encourage you to consider some longer periods of digital Sabbath.

One of the gifts of Sabbath rest is that it forces us to live within our limitations about how much we can consume. We can't listen to every podcast, watch every movie or TV show, or read every book or article. If we try to, we won't truly digest and process the information we consume. I can't tell you how many times someone brings up a book that it seems like *everyone* has read, except me. My initial reaction is feeling embarrassed and frustrated at myself for having a more limited capacity. Our minds are finite, and we need breathing room to process the content we choose to consume without feeling oversaturated.

LIFESTYLE OF REST

Our bodies and souls weren't designed to survive off a yearly vacation, yet that's how many of us are tempted to approach rest. If we want to flourish holistically, for the long term, we must learn to incorporate rest as a lifestyle. Many of us try to create habits of regular exercise, waking up at a certain time, or eating healthier foods. Just as we seek to create healthy habits for the rest of our lives, we should practice a regular rhythm of rest. I'd suggest pulling out a piece of paper and jotting down some ideas for rhythms of rest. Included on the list should be life-giving activities for your soul, your body, and your mind. If you have a spouse/kids, bring them into this practice. Below are some ideas for each.

Daily

- Set alarms on your phone throughout the day to remind you to pray.

- Listen to a psalm while you're cleaning up the house.
- Put your phone away at a certain time each evening. Don't pick it back up until a set time the next morning.
- Go to bed at a decent hour (simple, but many of us stay up far too late).
- Incorporate silence into your day. If you're in the car, don't rush to put on music or a podcast. If you're in the checkout line, don't pull out your phone to quickly check email, but notice and observe what's going on around you. Give your soul space to breath.

Weekly

- Observe a Sabbath.
- Host a weekly meal with your family or friends where you light candles, eat delicious food, and linger over long conversations.
- Step away from social media for a day.
- Spend time outside: go for a walk, a bike ride, or take your children to the playground.

Monthly

- Review your rhythms and note what's working for you and your family. Are you constantly staying up too late? Are you scrolling on your phone when you should be trying to fall asleep? It's much easier to make small, incremental changes than hit a breaking point and need to overhaul your entire life.
- Jot down your memories from the month. What were some of the sweetest moments? What were some challenges you faced? Take time to remember the Lord's faithfulness to you over the past month.

Yearly

- Consider a longer period of fasting from social media.
- Set aside some extended time to step away from work. You don't have to go on an extravagant vacation; you can stay home and explore your own town. But if you're able, try to have some extended time away from work.
- Set aside some extended time for reflection and preparation before a new year starts.

Pick and choose what works well for you. Each one of these suggestions are meant to get the ideas flowing. The goal is to grow into people who structure their lives to look like Jesus—to have time to grow in our knowledge and love for His Word, to serve the body of believers, and to pour out our lives for the kingdom of God.

CONCLUSION

I'm typing the final words of this chapter on another flight, headed to visit family again. The world is quiet, except the hum of the airplane and the clicking of my fingers on the keyboard. While my body is 30,000 feet in the air, my soul is rooted in rest. No meltdowns occurred on this flight; for that I'm grateful. The Lord was present with me then, and He's present now. As I've sought to prioritize rest and living within my limitations, I've put my phone away, gone to sleep at a decent hour, started taking long walks without headphones, and read more books for pleasure. The Lord has numbered our days, and I want to use mine well.

May we become women of deep abiding, living our lives from a place of rest with the Lord.

May we structure our lives in such a way that we rightly steward the good gifts the Lord has entrusted us with. May we make time to set down our phone, play with our children, look our friend in the eye over a cup of coffee, and give our full attention. May we learn to trust Him and find our true identity, worth, and rest in Him. Friend, whatever season you find yourself in today, I pray that you'll be encouraged to enter His rest today.

I want to close this chapter with a prayer from pastor Scotty Smith that I've returned to often, as I've sought to incorporate rhythms of rest into my life.

> Heavenly Father, nothing compares with the rest we have, being certain of your great love for us. No more wrestling with "he loves me, he loves me not"—for we now live in your permanent favor and unwavering delight. Jesus is our Sabbath Rest and Year of Jubilee; our mighty rock and loving refuge.
>
> Our honor and hope come from you, Father. They're not based on what people think or say of us; neither are they determined by our productivity or usefulness. Indeed, our honor and hope aren't connected to any scorecard, measuring stick, or annual review. Our standing in grace is inviolate, our rootedness in your love is deep, and hiddenness in Christ is complete. Hallelujah!
>
> Father, make these truths more real to us than our next breath. In fresh and palpable ways, be our refuge, rest, and hope. . . . We want to shake off slights, barbs, and quips quicker. We'd love to be more comfortable with unresolved issues, and the unhealed parts of our stories. Grant us longer fuses and shorter memories, in response to the failures of others and disappointments of our day.
>
> May your mercy tame our traumas, and your love sabotage our unbelief. Bring your grace to our frayed edges, messy stories, and yet-to-be known outcomes. It's a lot, Father, but we want *all* of these things. Thank you for being so

generous and able. So very Amen we pray, in Jesus' mercy-full and trust-worthy name.[14]

REFLECTION QUESTIONS

What would my life look like if I practiced regular rhythms of rest?

What does my obedience to a life of rest demonstrate to the world?

What areas of my life do I need to live within my own limitations?

What are the next steps of implementation I'm going to take after reading this chapter?

FURTHER READING

The Ruthless Elimination of Hurry: How to Stay Emotionally Healthy and Spiritually Alive in the Chaos of the Modern World—John Mark Comer[15]

Sacred Rhythms: Arranging Our Lives for Spiritual Transformation—Ruth Haley Barton[16]

You're Only Human: How Your Limits Reflect God's Design and Why That's Good News—Kelly Kapic[17]

SCRIPTURE TO MEDITATE UPON

"Be still before the Lord and wait patiently for him; fret not yourself over the one who prospers in his way, over the man who carries out evil devices!"

—Ps. 37:7

"You keep him in perfect peace whose mind is stayed on you, because he trusts in you."

—Isa. 26:3

"For thus said the Lord God, the Holy One of Israel, 'In returning and rest you shall be saved; in quietness and in trust shall be your strength.'"

—Isa. 30:15

"Be still, and know that I am God. I will be exalted among the nations, I will be exalted in the earth!"

—Ps. 46:10

Chapter 9

Can Women Have It All?

A Grace-Filled Approach to Productivity

Take my life, and let it be consecrated, Lord, to thee.
Take my moments and my days; let them flow in ceaseless praise.

Frances R. Havergal[1]

How do you do it all?*

This might be one of the most frequent questions women ask one another, as they are struggling to figure out how to align their calendars, to-do lists, goals, and desires. We look at others, thinking they must have it all together and that we don't have what it takes. We envy the working mom, who seems to always have time to squeeze in a workout and have a healthy dinner on the table by six o'clock each evening. We scroll social media and see the women who've started their own companies and have the ability to take time off to travel, and we wonder how it doesn't all fall apart without them at the helm. Women seem to cheerfully maintain clean and tidy homes and never lose their patience with their children.

We look around us and wonder how other women seem to balance everything so perfectly, when we feel like we're constantly dropping the ball. Books have been written answering this question and providing us with techniques and tips for maximizing productivity and living lives of passion, all while maintaining a cheerful spirit and a happy family. At the core of these questions, what I think we're really asking is, "How can I make the most of this one life that I've been given?" We look for the secret sauce, the magic formula that'll tell us the exact steps we need to take to achieve the life we want.

The reality is, no one can "do it all"—at least, not at one time. The idea of balance implies that we can and should be giving the same amount of attention to all areas of our lives, but not every area of our lives deserves equal attention. We can't give equal attention to all areas of our life at once—something must give.

When I wrote my first book, I was working a full-time job on Capitol Hill, planning a wedding, and squeezing writing into the margins. Currently, I'm writing this book while still working full time and going through the international adoption process with my husband. Plenty of people have asked me how I've done it. The honest answer is lots of sacrifice. This morning, I got up at 5:30 a.m. to write until I needed to head into work. I've sacrificed vacation days and used them to work on my manuscript. I've sacrificed by saying no to good opportunities, so that I can say yes to what I've committed to. Writing this book and stewarding this message were deeply important to me, and it has been worth the sacrifices I made.

Rather than seeking to balance everything, think of stewarding your assignments and responsibilities like riding a bike. In order to "balance" riding a bike, your weight must constantly be shifting. The same goes with our lives. I've spoken much about seasons of life throughout this book. That concept comes into sharp focus in this chapter. Our seasons will dictate where the "weight" of our time, energy, and attention go.

ON LIVING IN THE LORD'S TIME

Writing this chapter felt paradoxical for me; on one hand, I love reading about productivity and time management. I love setting goals and strategizing about how to best use my limited time. On the other hand,

I often struggle with time anxiety, "the terrible feeling that [I] never have enough time and [am not] doing enough with the time [I] *do* have."[2] This struggle with time often provokes an anxiousness and restlessness within me. I often feel as if there's never enough time, and I want to perfectly manage my time, and not waste a second of this one precious life. Far too many of us know just how fleeting life is. As the saying goes: *The days are long, but the years are short.* We know that time is an unrenewable resource that slips away all too quickly.

Time management, as Jen Pollock Michel writes, is "the premise of control . . . *you* are working to achieve *your* best life now."[3] But we end our days often reminded of how little control we actually have. Our to-do lists are longer by the end of the day than at the beginning. We crawl into bed exhausted, reminded of all the things left undone. We chase the mirage of control, but ultimately find that it's just a vapor.

The psalmist cries, "Teach us to number our days that we may get a heart of wisdom."[4] His prayer for an attentive heart to the brevity of time is a prayer for *wisdom*, not a prayer for *productivity*.

We should be intentional about how we manage and steward our time. But rather than focusing on productivity, for the sake of getting more done, we should focus more on seeking wisdom—and wisdom can't often be measured. Psalm 1 gives us a picture of a blessed and righteous man and tells us the secret to a happy and fruitful life.

> *Blessed* is the man who walks not in the counsel of the wicked, nor stands in the way of sinners, nor sits in the seat of scoffers; but his delight is in the law of the LORD, and on his law he meditates day and night. He is like a tree planted by streams of water *that yields its fruit in its season*, and its leaf does not wither. In all that he does, he prospers.[5]

The Greek word translated "blessed" is "*makarioi* which means to be fully satisfied. It refers to those receiving God's favor, *regardless of the circumstances*."[6] Scripture holds up a model for us to pattern our lives after and tells us the secret to a blessed life. The man in Psalm 1 is deeply rooted and planted and seeking a life of holiness. Rather than focusing on productivity, Psalm 1 focuses on fruitfulness. The blessed man is like a tree, and the thing about trees is they often take a long time to form deep roots and produce good fruit.

Christians should fundamentally understand and observe time differently because we know that we're "living on the Lord's time." This ought to free us up from the relentless pursuit of cramming every minute with productivity. We can welcome interruptions in our schedule and linger over coffee with a friend, because she needs our presence and attention. As we've discussed throughout the book, the calling of our lives is to love God and love our neighbor. But the thing about love is that you can't often love in a hurry. You can optimize your life for a lot of things, but love requires slowing down, setting down your devices, and offering your attention and presence. Love requires honoring your limitations and capacities, because to truly love others, you must give your time, energy, and attention.

THE WOMAN YOU'RE BECOMING

Ephesians 5:16 tells us to make the best use of the time. Our time on earth is finite; therefore we must carefully choose how we'll spend our limited time, energy, and attention. Rather than seeking to do it all, we should identify what matters most to *us*. As author Jordan Raynor writes, "Jesus understood his purpose, and that allowed him to take the long list of things he *could* do and pare it down to the things he knew he *should* do to finish the work the Father gave him to do (see John 17:4)."[7] As we seek to live in the Lord's time, rather than the world's, a helpful exercise is to step back and think about the type of woman you want to become. I encourage you to take out a sheet of paper and journal through some of these questions:

- What do you want your legacy to be?
- What type of woman do you want to be at eighty?
- What are some areas of your life you need to surrender to the Lord?
- Who in your life can you actively be loving, serving, and sharing the gospel with?
- How can you love and serve your family? Your neighbors? Your local church community?

Allow yourself to think and pray through those questions. And then work backward from there. What do you need to change today to help you become that woman?

I'm often tempted to think that one more time management book or well implemented system will help me become the woman I want to be. It always feels like the secret to the good life is just one more self-help book away. While I have read some books that have been helpful in my life, recently I've tended to shy away from those types of books because of how they make me feel—not enough.

The truth is, we *are* lacking and needy, but the answer isn't to turn to ourselves. If we were able to perfectly manage our lives, we wouldn't be aware of our weakness and need for the Lord's strength and guidance. We're not supposed to live in our own strength. In Scripture, we are reminded that apart from God, we can do nothing (John 15:5), and we're called to live in the Spirit, not the flesh (Rom. 8:1–11). All our lives should be viewed as an offering to the Lord, and we should readily invite the Holy Spirit into every single area of our lives and allow His power to be made perfect in our weakness (2 Cor. 12:9).

As we seek to become godly, faithful women who steward our lives well, it can be tempting to believe that we must make bold, dramatic changes in our lives and in the world around us. But nothing can be further from the truth. Small acts of faithfulness add up to a faithful life. The good life is found in joyfully obeying the Lord and in stewarding our lives well, for our good and His glory.

For some people, the reality of how short life is terrifies them, and they spend their lives pursuing wealth, accolades, achievements, and pleasure. But on the other hand, for those who are in Christ, we should structure our lives differently. We are freed from relentlessly pursuing fame, finances, and fun. Our stories don't end when we die—we have been promised eternity with our King. This good news means that we don't have to cram as much as possible into our lives on earth, because our stories will continue. We can now joyfully steward our time, talent, and treasure for the glory of God and our neighbor.

IT'S OKAY NOT TO BALANCE EVERYTHING

Glass Balls vs. Plastic Balls

My dear friend Sarah shared this analogy with me, and I want to pass it along to you. Think of the different spheres in your life as plastic and glass balls. Some balls are plastic and will bounce back if we drop them or set them aside for a particular season. Other balls are glass, and if we drop them, they will shatter and be difficult to repair. Identify what your glass balls are and protect those first and foremost. For many people, their glass balls are relationships—with God, with family, friends, and their church community.

Some examples of plastic balls might be: how elaborate your meals are (peanut butter fills the belly just as well as a more elaborate meal) or how tidy your home is at a given time. Everyone's glass and plastic balls will be different, but it's important to think through which balls we can afford to drop. Dropping a ball or intentionally setting it aside for a season doesn't mean that we'll neglect it forever. But in a particular season, we might have to make some tough choices. Below are some spheres to consider and prayerfully think through:

Spiritual
- Personal relationship with the Lord
- Memorizing Scripture
- Time in prayer

Community
- Immediate family
- Extended family
- Friends
- Small group
- Church community

Health
- Physical health
- Fueling our bodies well
- Getting enough sleep
- Mental health
- Emotional health

Financial
- Regular budget meetings
- Generosity to others
- Saving intentionally for the future

Vocational
- Professional development
- Knowledge acquisition
- Networking

Intellectual Life
- Education
- Reading
- Pursuing hobbies

My relationship with my husband is a glass ball in my life. I want to structure my time and energy in such a way that he always knows that he's a top priority to me. We do this by trying to regularly set aside intentional time for us to connect and share our inner lives with one another. But there are short seasons of my professional life that are unusually busy, and I won't be able to spend as much time with him. I try to communicate well ahead of time that it's an unusual week and share that I might need some extra help at home or extra margin. We both know that this is the exception, and not the rule. I'm not dropping my glass ball because it's not a habit.

To properly prioritize our glass balls in unusual seasons (busy seasons at work, times of illness, or caring for a family member), it's helpful to figure out what plastic balls you can drop so that your glass balls can continue to be prioritized and well cared for.

There might be times when it feels like everything is a priority, and every time you sit down to work on something, you're overwhelmed and paralyzed by the ten other things that you should be doing. If you're feeling that way, figure out if you can ask someone for help. Maybe you ask your small group to watch the kids for an evening while you have a night to catch your breath. Maybe you eat freezer meals all week to ease the burden of cooking, or maybe you simplify your routines for a season.

GRACE-FILLED APPROACH TO PRODUCTIVITY

The way we choose to spend our time, energy, and attention is ultimately a way to love our families, friends, and communities well. But these things don't happen by chance. We don't accidentally become more like Christ—it requires time, energy, work, a reliance upon the Holy Spirit, and a life of prayer. We don't accidentally love our neighbor—it takes forethought, planning, and execution.

The Proverbs 31 woman shows us a woman who fears the Lord and works diligently out of love for her family and community. We're given insight into how this woman plans and produces. She rises while it is yet night, provides food for her household, prepares ahead to clothe her family for the winter, and opens her hand to the poor. Productivity marked her life, but she did it out of love for others.

The goal of productivity is to approach all of life as a steward. In his book *Do More Better*, Tim Challies states that "productivity is effectively stewarding your gifts, talents, time, energy, and enthusiasm for the good of others and the glory of God."[8] He goes on to say that "God calls you to productivity, but he calls you to the right kind of productivity. He calls you to be productive for his sake, not your own." The world's view of productivity is to elevate yourself above everyone else. But a stewardship mindset understands that different seasons of life will demand different things from us. We plan, steward, and are faithful, but we trust the Lord when we fall. While I do believe Scripture calls us to be wise about stewarding our time, our identity should always be rooted in Christ's finished work for us on the cross.

Many of us know that we ought to budget our financial resources, but we should also have a similar mindset to how we budget our time, energy, and attention—all of which are limited resources. Our time on this earth isn't infinite, and none of us know when our last breath might be. We should seek to have an eternity mindset with all our resources.

RHYTHMS AND ROUTINES

Books have been written on subjects such as the power of habit, atomic habits, habits of the household. Authors repeatedly remind us of the importance of habits: "a settled or regular tendency or behavior."[9] We become what we regularly behold and practice. Our habits make up our lives and can help us to love God and others well. For many of us, we can get overwhelmed by all the decisions we have to make. One of the ways we can help eliminate decision fatigue is by setting up some rhythms and routines that serve us well. By creating routines for certain tasks or areas of our lives, we're able to free up more mental and emotional space for things that matter more.

Rather than giving you five steps to success, or the "perfect" morning routine of a successful person, I want to give you a better, more life-giving tool: enter rhythms. Rhythms help us focus more on who we're *becoming* than what goals we are achieving. Rhythms aren't rigid and can change and be flexible as you enter into different seasons of your life. They are meant to be life-giving, not draining.

Let's take exercise as an example. Most of us know that regular exercise is good for us physically, emotionally, and mentally. But many of us often struggle with regular exercise. Why? Because the desire to care well for our bodies, lose a few pounds, or tone up often takes a back seat to the more seemingly urgent and important tasks in our lives. We bemoan the fact that we "don't have time," but what gets scheduled gets done.

What would happen if you developed an exercise routine?

You might not be a naturally disciplined person, and the thought of a routine makes your skin crawl. Hear me out. What if you simply decided ahead of time that you're going to go for a jog on M/W/F? There you go—you have your exercise routine and all you must do now is follow the plan you've laid out. When life gets busy, and you skip a Monday or a week's worth of workouts, you don't have to reinvent the wheel or decide how to exercise, all you have to do is reengage with the rhythm you've already set up.

Rhythms and routines are a pathway to freedom. Not only do they free up mental capacity once we've decided ahead of time how we're going to spend our time, but they provide a set of boundaries we structure our lives around. The good news is you can build a routine around anything. Want to prioritize more family time? Sit down and sketch out what success looks like to you in this area. Maybe for you, it's eating dinner together most nights and having a movie and pizza night on Fridays. Great! That's your rhythm for family time. Of course, you can always adjust it as your seasons change. But this is a starting block and a foundation from which to build.

Or maybe your job requires you to become an expert at a topic. Block off a set amount of time to work on a particular goal. Maybe you begin by writing three days a week, for an hour each day. Or maybe your goal is to write five hundred words every day. The possibilities are endless. The goal isn't perfection. You won't honor your rhythms all the time, but they are there as guardrails for your life. When you have a good rhythm for something, even if you get off track for a few days or weeks, the good news is, you can pick right back up where you left off.

Rhythms and routines don't have to be complicated or complex. You don't need a 12-step morning routine; figure out what's life-giving for you and your family, and work from there. You also don't have to be beholden to your rhythms and routines if they aren't serving you well any longer. One of the rhythms you can develop is to regularly examine your rhythms. Maybe every quarter, you sit down and examine what's working well and what's not. What routines need to be tweaked for the upcoming season? Be realistic and honest with where you are.

Here are some examples of some rhythms and routines you might want to create or reevaluate:

- Morning routine
- Evening routine
- Cleaning routine
- Meal planning routine
- Routines for friendship

- Routines for reading
- Exercise routine
- Weekly planning routine

How do you start creating a routine? Sit down and think through what an ideal scenario would look like. From there, begin drafting up what you'd like a certain routine to look like. For example, here's what my morning routine looks like: wake up, make coffee, and spend time journaling, reading Scripture, and praying, then I shower and get ready for the day. I can usually have some form of this rhythm, even if I wake up later than I intended. All I have to do is shorten it. Don't overcomplicate this, and remember that life happens and it's okay to give yourself grace.

In addition to the rhythms and routines that help keep our lives running smoothly, many of us need a way to manage the incoming papers, messages, to-do list items, etc. It's helpful to build a personal productivity system. These can be as simple or elaborate as you'd like, but the basics will help us.

BUILDING YOUR OWN PRODUCTIVITY SYSTEM

Most of us live in a culture where there are usually five thousand demands for our time and attention. We might either feel the need to double down and work around the clock to "get it all done," or we might throw up our hands and declare that it's too difficult. Even if you don't get a thrill out of productivity and organization, I believe that everyone can benefit from a personal productivity system. The good news is this doesn't have to be an elaborate or intricate system. Some people are up-to-date with the latest technology and can skillfully navigate the most sophisticated apps. Others prefer pen and paper, and some use a hybrid system of both. The tool isn't what matters most. What matters is that a productivity system serves you, not for you to be a slave to technology or your system. Our system doesn't have to be elaborate or terribly time consuming, but we do need to develop a way you can regularly tame the demands on our time and attention so we can rightly prioritize what matters most in life.

Our brains weren't built to keep all our tasks, appointments, and random bits of information stored in them. When we have a well-developed system for capturing those pieces of information, it frees our brains up to think about other things, and we won't constantly feel like we're forgetting something. Having a productivity system actually frees up our mental capacities.

The three pillars of a productivity system are a calendar, a way to manage your tasks, and a way to store and manage information and important documents. Not only do these systems help us not forget a birthday or milk at the grocery store, but they can also be utilized to better love our neighbors and our communities.

Calendar

You need a way to capture appointments, birthdays, anniversary, and due dates. A calendar is how we manage our time and remember our commitments. Personally, I use Google Calendar and Michael Hyatt's Full Focus Planner system. I like a hybrid system because I'm able to quickly throw appointments on the calendar and easily adjust without too much hassle. Additionally, I can share my calendars with certain people or invite my husband to my appointments so he's aware of what's going on in my day. I use the Full Focus Planner to drill down and plan my days and my weeks.

The most important thing to remember about maintaining a calendar is to immediately add things to it. Did you just lock in coffee with a friend? Throw it on the calendar as soon as you schedule it. I can't tell you how many times I've thought I'll remember to add something later, and then I completely forget. Or, I feel stressed trying to remember the information until I actually write it down. Add in as much information as you can: date, time, location, Zoom link, meeting notes, dress code, guest list, etc.

When we get into the habit of regularly adding everything to our calendar and reviewing our commitments, we must be honest with ourselves and our families about how much we can and should be committing to. We should seek to be thoughtful with our commitments so that we're able to rightly order and steward our time for the things that matter most. Go back to the vision of the type of woman you want to be. Is she always in a hurry and rushed, or does she have time to be interrupted?

Our calendar also reflects our priorities. Author Annie Dillard has this helpful wisdom about how we spend our time:

> How we spend our days is, of course, how we spend our lives. What we do with this hour, and that one, is what we are doing. A schedule defends from chaos and whim. It is a net for catching days. It is a scaffolding on which a worker can stand and labor with both hands at sections of time. A schedule is a mock-up of reason and order—willed, faked, and so brought into being; it is a peace and a haven set into the wreck of time; it is a lifeboat on which you find yourself, decades later, still living. Each day is the same, so you remember the series afterward as a blurred and powerful pattern.[10]

Different seasons of life will demand different things from us. Be gracious with yourself if you need to scale back during certain seasons. It might be tempting to compare, but each of us has certain capacities and limitations. Be in constant prayer over your calendar and what goes on it.

Review your calendar a week in advance. When you do this, you can take a few moments to confirm plans with people, drop birthday cards in the mail for friends and family, and see any potential conflicts and quickly deal with them before it becomes an emergency. I also encourage you to review your calendar the day before too. This takes me less than two minutes but helps me think through the next day. I've also caught things I'd forgotten about.

Task Manager

Has this ever happened to you? You use up the last of the milk in the refrigerator, make a mental note, but the next time you're at the store, forget to pick up milk. As David Allen, the author of *Getting Things Done*, reminds us: "Your brain is for having ideas, not storing them."[11]

Just like capturing your appointments on your calendar, get in the habit of regularly writing down to-do list items, reminders, things to follow up on, etc. If you jot something down as soon as you think of it, you'll free up mental energy that can be better used elsewhere.

This process needs to be as painless and easy as possible so that you'll actually follow through and write something down. Again, I personally like a hybrid system because I don't always have pen and paper with me, but I usually have my phone with me. I can quickly add something on the Reminders app on my phone, or jot down a quick note. There's no right or wrong way to keep up with your tasks. Experiment with different things until you find what works well for you.

Information and Documents

We need a system and way to manage our personal and important documents—both hard copies and virtual documents. Personally, I use both Google Drive and Evernote. It's so helpful to have everything stored electronically because I'm able to cut back on paper and quickly and painlessly find everything. You don't have to be super organized to maintain your documents online; the search features are so powerful, you can typically find everything pretty easily.

Weekly Planning

One of the rhythms that's been enormously beneficial for me is a weekly planning session. I'll be honest, when I first heard about this concept, I put off trying it for a while. It sounded overwhelming or like it was going to take hours of my time each week. A weekly planning session doesn't have to be elaborate or complex, but I've found that it pays back huge dividends.

Here's an idea of some things you can review in your weekly planning session.

- Calendar
- Finances
- To-do list (this is also when you can glance through the Reminders app and notes section of your phone, to make sure you didn't overlook anything)
- Catch up on emails
- Catch up on texts and social media messages

Once you set up these systems, you need a way to regularly stay on top of them, so they don't get completely out of control.

How to Use These Tools to Love and Serve Others

- Add events to pray for on your calendar—a family member's surgery, a difficult conversation that's been scheduled, etc.
- Add your friend's birthdays onto your calendar and a reminder for a week out so that you can drop them a card in the mail.
- Add other memorable days in your friends' lives—maybe the day a parent passed away, so you can reach out to them annually and let them know you're praying for them.

- Plan out ways to regularly serve others. I keep a few items on hand for gifts and keep a well-supplied stationery drawer. I also have a few meals that are relatively cheap and can be adapted to different dietary restrictions and needs. Additionally, I keep some inexpensive Tupperware on hand for delivering meals. I get them on sale at Walmart or Target for under $5, and it removes the stress for both parties from figuring how and when to return the dishes.

TECHNOLOGY

Developing and maintaining good technology boundaries is like taking your vitamins—you know it's good for you, and you know you should, but it's not usually fun or enjoyable. But as we discussed earlier, observing limitations is often the way to greater freedom. The same applies to our use of technology, our phones, and social media.

Turn off notifications on your phone and computer. Seriously. Trust me on this one. I turned off all notifications on my phone except for texts and calls a long time ago, and it's been one of the best decisions I've ever made. The reality is we don't need to be notified every time someone likes a photo of ours on Instagram or a relative comments on our Facebook post. Decide what your tech boundaries will be and try to stick to them.

This is an area I have to admit that I constantly struggle with. I've had seasons where I feel like I'm honoring my boundaries extremely well and seasons where I hardly know what a boundary is. But I think it's important for us to know what we want a relationship with technology to be. An easy first step is to sleep with your phone in another room. If you're afraid you'll miss an important phone call, put it on the other side of the room and only allow certain people to call through. Sleep with an old-school alarm clock, so that the first thing you do when you wake up isn't checking your phone.

The most important thing I want you to walk away with is that there's no "one size fits all" approach to productivity, time management, and organization. Each one of us is living in a different season, with different demands on our time, energy, and emotions. It's okay if you're not a member of the 5 a.m. club and your closet isn't color coordinated. Those things might matter to some people, but if they don't matter to you, great! Don't force yourself to do something or be someone you're not, just because you saw it on Instagram.

THE PROMISE OF MORE TIME

One of the promises of eternity that we will have more time—an abundance of time. Psalm 1 tells us that the blessed man is "like a tree planted by streams of water." In the last chapter of the Bible, Scripture tells us about "the river of the water of life . . . and on either side of the river, the tree of life."[12]

Psalm 1 is not only perfectly fulfilled in the work of Jesus, it points us to the New Jerusalem. As we go about our moments and our days, as we rest in our calling to faithfully obey the Lord and tend to the assignments entrusted to our care, may we do so with our gaze fixed on eternity. This life matters, but it's not all there is. Our work has eternal value, but one day soon we will "enter into his rest."[13]

There is a day coming when God will dwell with His people, and He will wipe away every tear from our eyes and there will be no more pain.[14] Our earthly toil and trouble will be ultimately redeemed, and we will worship and work in redeemed bodies.

Thanks be to God.

May we be women who live a deep, purposeful, and intentional life. May we be women who strive to faithfully steward our time, talent, and attention well. May we have margin for the meaningful moments of life. May we devote ourselves to glorifying the Lord and loving His people. May we grow into godly women. May we work hard in advancing God's kingdom, the common good, and the flourishing of others.

REFLECTION QUESTIONS

What are the most important things in this season of life for me to focus on?

How can I view productivity to love God and serve others?

How can I best structure my time to ensure I'm giving my energy and focus to the things that matter most?

What are the most important things I'm going to implement from this chapter?

FURTHER READING

What's Best Next: How the Gospel Transforms the Way You Get Things Done—Matt Perman[15]

Do More Better: A Practical Guide to Productivity—Tim Challies[16]

The Common Rule: Habits of Purpose for an Age of Distraction—Justin Whitmel Earley[17]

SCRIPTURE TO MEDITATE UPON

"Look carefully then how you walk, not as unwise but as wise, making the best use of the time, because the days are evil."

—*Eph. 5:15–16*

"The soul of the sluggard craves and gets nothing, while the soul of the diligent is richly supplied."

—Prov. 13:4

"The plans of the diligent lead surely to abundance, but everyone who is hasty comes only to poverty."

—Prov. 21:5

"Whoever works his land will have plenty of bread, but he who follows worthless pursuits lacks sense."

—Prov. 12:11

"In all toil there is profit, but mere talk tends only to poverty."

—Prov. 14:23

"How long will you lie there, O sluggard? When will you arise from your sleep? A little sleep, a little slumber, a little folding of the hands to rest, and poverty will come upon you like a robber, and want like an armed man."

—Prov. 6:9–11

Afterword

As I close this book, I wanted to share a deeply personal reflection upon my own work. I often feel like I'm standing on the edge of the sea with a teaspoon. The quicker I scoop out teaspoons of water, the quicker the ocean seems to fill back up. I want so desperately for my life and my work to matter and make a difference. I want my teaspoons of effort and energy to make a tangible impact on the lives around me. I didn't long for a spotlight, but I do long to make the world better than I found it. I'm deeply motivated by correcting injustices and casting light into darkness. Much of my professional life has been working on behalf of vulnerable people—whether it's vulnerable children, persecuted people around the world, or refugees fleeing danger. There's so much need in the world, and my effort feels minuscule most days.

But the Lord is teaching me that my teaspoons of work matter. They matter because He called and equipped me for that work. My small teaspoons of work image God to a hurting world. When I collapse into bed, exhausted by the day's work, frustrated that I couldn't do more, and burdened by the sorrows I've encountered, I'm reminded that nothing is hidden from God's sight. History will only remember a handful of names. But we are known deeply to our Father. Isaiah tells us, "Behold, I have engraved you on the palms of my hands" (Isa. 49:16). Charles Spurgeon provides this beautiful meditation on this verse.

> He cries, "How can I have forgotten you, when I have engraved you on the palms of My hands? The name is there, but that is not all: "I have engraved you." Consider the depth of this! "I have engraved your person, your image, your circumstances, your sins, your temptations, your weaknesses, your wants, your works; I have engraved you, everything about you, all that concerns you; I have put all of this together here."[1]

Last year, my husband, Michael, surprised me with a poem. I'd told him about the feeling of standing on the edge of the sea with my teaspoon, and he beautifully put words to that image. I'd like to close the book with this poem. I pray that if you've struggled with similar feelings, these words would encourage your soul, to remember that your work does matter, for the King.

THE GIRL AND THE SEA
By Michael Sobolik

There is a girl
At the edge of the world
With a spoon in her hand

...

Kneeling down at water's brink
She scoops and scoops
Water dripping, water running
From sea to spoon to pail

...

Over and over and over again

...

From dusk to dawn
From then to now
For her whole life long
The girl on earth's edge scoops

...

Her heart so big, her spoon so small
The girl knows the game
The sea, her enemy, the father of all things wrong
Scorns her scoops and never shrinks

...

Still she ladles away
For strangers in danger and family catastrophes
Her bucket catches the lonely and the bruised
Shelters them and tends their wounds

...

A good day here, a good day there
But the nights haunt her dreams
Of the ones she didn't touch
Of those she couldn't reach

...

The world on her shoulders
Though her feet touch the ground
Her heart so big, but not so strong
For all that was lost to be found

...

Then one night the voice of a kinder Father
Spoke gently in her sleep

And silenced the sea
Shut up its lies from the deep

…

The Father spoke, but no words came
He breathed a picture on her soul
There she sat in another's bucket
Far away from the mocking shoal

…

Someone scooped her, she knew not who
But by someone's heart and another's spoon
She was rescued and delivered
From the dark side of the moon

…

"My girl, my girl," the Father whispered,
Do you not see my plan?
You are not meant to drain the waters
For who alone but I can?
Yes one day, my darling daughter
I will part sea from infinity to infinity
There will be no ocean or moon
In the paradise of my vicinity
Whether by angels, man, or kitty cats
You are always held and kept
In my preserving power
From which none shall intercept
For now, as you hold pain and grief
And scoop away to heal doom
Know that I hold you, my beloved
And scoop you up with my spoon

…

When the girl awoke she felt
A peace had settled overnight
Not from strength of spoon or pail
But from her Father's sweet delight

I am held,

she gently sighed

I am held from now to then
My bucket and spoon so small—but God
Holds all pain—even mine. Amen.

. . .

There is a girl
At the edge of the world
With a spoon in her hand

. . .

She scoops and scoops and scoops again
Not in fear but hope, she simply tries
To hold and love the ones nearby
Until her Father drains the ocean dry[2]

Acknowledgments

Here's a little secret about me—almost every time I crack open a new book, I immediately flip to the dedication and acknowledgments. I love reading the names of the people who helped shape an author's message, who loved and supported them as they wrote, and who are meaningful to their lives.

Many of these people deserve to have their names on the front of the book alongside an author's because they are so deeply invested in the author and their message. So, while it's nearly impossible to properly thank everyone, I am grateful that this section exists, so I can begin to express my gratitude.

First, thank you! I'm truly so grateful that you spent your precious time, energy, and attention reading my book. Thousands of books fill the shelves in bookstores, libraries, and online, and you chose to invest in mine. This honor isn't lost on me, and I'm deeply thankful.

To my agent, Ingrid Beck—thank you for being one of the first people to believe in this book and for representing it so well.

To Trillia Newbell, Catherine Parks, and Amanda Cleary Eastep—thank you for skillfully stewarding and shaping this book. I have the utmost respect and gratitude for you three.

To Timothy and Kathy Keller, Katherine Leary Alsdorf, Joanna Meyer, Elyse Fitzpatrick, Eric Schumacher, Jen Wilkin, Dorothy Sayers, Steven Garber, Amy Sherman, Justin Whitmel Earley, John Mark Comer, and Jen Pollock Michel—you all shaped and sharpened my thinking on the topics of work, calling, vocation, rest, and rhythms. Thank you for obeying the calling God laid on your heart.

To my dear friends who have faithfully walked alongside me, believed in me, held my arms up when I grew weary, encouraged me, and loved me—Rachel Procopio, Amanda Sanders, Alexandria Paolozzi, Ericka Morris, Lauren Devoll, Genta Arnold, John Botello, Sarah Bradshaw, Joylane Bartron, Seth and Melika McKinnis, Danny and Maddy Huizenga, Olivia Enos, Tori Smith, Ruth Malhotra, Brittany Salmon, Ken Farnaso, Kristina Baum, and Lauren McAfee.

To my bosses and coworkers throughout the years—you all made me a better person and better employee. I am grateful to have served alongside you all—Kenda Bartlett, Jonathan Hayes, Russell Moore, Brent Leatherwood, Travis Wussow, Herbie Newell, Rick Morton, Chris Johnson, Bethany Haley, Andy Braun, Lydia Taylor, Melissa Elledge, Bobby Cornett, Mitch Hailstone, Jeff Pickering, Steven Harris, Brooke Kramer, Lauren Dalton, Palmer Williams, Julie Masson, Hannah Daniel, Elizabeth Graham, Josh Wester, Alex Ward, Jason Thacker, Conrad Close, Marie Delph, Amanda Hays, Lauren Brown, Bobby Reed, Stacey Keck, Tom Strode, Rachel Wiles, Karla Thrasher, Skip Stallings, Lesley Scott, Traci Newell, Tim Crist, Aren Williams, and Rebecca Lentner.

To my family—Bobby and Christie Patterson, Mike and Liz Sobolik, Lindsey and James Sobolik-Williams, Nicholas and Raven Patterson, Alaina and Jason Espeneoza, Alexander Patterson, Chloe Patterson. I love you all more than words can convey.

To my dearest Michael—thank you for selflessly loving me, for carrying the burden when I needed strength. You have my heart, always.

To my son—how loved you already are. I pray that you will grasp the Father's love for you, and you will grow up learning the dignity and value of work, while remembering that your ultimate worth and identity are always found in Christ.

Ultimately, this book is an offering to my God—the One who designed us to be a working people, the One who sent His Son to redeem and rescue, the One who promises never to leave or forsake us, and the One who will wipe away our tears and dwell with us forever. Soli Deo gloria.

Notes

CHAPTER 1: DESIGNED TO WORK

1. Timothy Keller and Katherine Leary Alsdorf, *Every Good Endeavor: Connecting Your Work to God's Work* (New York: Dutton, 2012), 48.
2. Jenna Goudreau, "Find Happiness At Work," *Forbes*, March 4, 2010, https://www.forbes.com/2010/03/04/happiness-work-resilience-forbes-woman-well-being-satisfaction.html.
3. Genesis 1:1–25.
4. The Gospel Coalition, "Imago Dei in Creation and Fall | Session 1," February 28, 2022, YouTube video, https://www.youtube.com/watch?v=8V50vtmNISw.
5. Kathy Keller, "Called to Be a Woman," *Q Ideas* podcast, episode 234, March 10, 2022, https://podcasts.apple.com/us/podcast/episode-234-called-to-be-a-woman-kathy-keller/id1072608281?i=1000553608950.
6. Ibid.
7. Genesis 1:31.
8. William Edgar, "The Creation Mandate," The Gospel Coalition, https://www.thegospelcoalition.org/essay/the-creation-mandate/.
9. Dictionary.com, s.v. "dominion (*n.*)," https://www.dictionary.com/browse/dominion.
10. Keller and Alsdorf, *Every Good Endeavor*, 48.
11. Richard Phillips, "The Origin of Sin," The Gospel Coalition, https://www.thegospelcoalition.org/essay/the-origin-of-sin/.
12. Footnote in *ESV Study Bible* (Wheaton, IL: Crossway, 2008), 56.
13. Timothy Keller, *The Reason for God: Belief in an Age of Skepticism* (New York: Penguin Books, 2018), 183.

14. 2 Corinthians 5:18.
15. Jeff Haanen, "Why Faith & Work?," Denver Institute for Faith & Work, https://denverinstitute.org/why/.
16. Dictionary.com, s.v. "cultivate (*v.*)," https://www.dictionary.com/browse/cultivate.
17. Melissa Kruger, "Sisters, You Have Permission to Lead an Ordinary Life," The Gospel Coalition, October 1, 2020, www.thegospelcoalition.org/article/permission-lead-ordinary-life/.
18. Timothy Keller and Katherine Leary Alsdorf, *Every Good Endeavor: Connecting Your Work to God's Work* (New York: Dutton, 2012).

CHAPTER 2: BIBLICAL PATTERNS FOR WOMEN AND WORK

1. Elyse Fitzpatrick and Eric Schumacher, *Worthy: Celebrating the Value of Women* (Minneapolis: Bethany House, 2020), 27.
2. Elisabeth Elliot, *Let Me Be a Woman* (Wheaton, IL: Tyndale House Publishers, 2004), 45.
3. Fitzpatrick and Schumacher, *Worthy*, 18.
4. Ibid.
5. Genesis 2:20.
6. Jen Wilkin, "Are Compatibility and Complementarity at Odds?," Jen Wilkin (blog), March 29, 2016, https://www.jenwilkin.net/blog/2016/03/are-compatibility-and-complementarity.html.
7. "Lexicon: Strong's H5828 ʻ*ēzer*," Blue Letter Bible, https://www.blueletterbible.org/lexicon/h5828/kjv/wlc/0-1/.
8. Many thanks to Elyse Fitzpatrick and Eric Schumacher and their book *Worthy* for these observations.
9. Eric Schumacher, "21 Places Women Emerge Front and Center in Scripture's Storyline," The Gospel Coalition, June 2, 2018, https://www.thegospelcoalition.org/article/21-places-women-emerge-front-and-center-in-scriptures-storyline/.
10. See Romans 8:29.
11. Matthew 28:16–20 and Matthew 22:36–40.
12. Proverbs 31:13–20.

13. Fitzpatrick and Schumacher, *Worthy*, 18.
14. Made to Flourish, "Flourishing Culture—Andy Crouch," August 26, 2020, YouTube video, https://www.youtube.com/watch?v=jQID8QioRcc.
15. Susan Milligan, "Timeline: The Women's Rights Movement in the US," *US News & World Report*, March, 10, 2023, https://www.usnews.com/news/the-report/articles/2017-01-20/timeline-the-womens-rights-movement-in-the-us.
16. Kristin Corey, "Arabella (Belle) Babb Mansfield, First Certified Female Attorney in the United States," Iowa Department of Cultural Affairs, August 18, 2020, https://iowaculture.gov/history/education/educator-resources/primary-source-sets/government-democracy-and-laws/arabella.
17. *Bradwell v. The State* (The US Supreme Court, April 15, 1873).
18. "All About Anna," Bissell.com, June 29, 2017, https://www.bissell.com/blog/bissell-blog/all-about-anna.html.
19. Christine M. Kreiser, "The First Minimum Wage," HistoryNet, June 2, 2014, https://www.historynet.com/the-first-minimum-wage/.
20. "Women in Congress," US House of Representatives: History, Art & Archives, https://history.house.gov/Education/Fact-Sheets/WIC-Fact-Sheet2/.
21. "19th Amendment to the US Constitution: Women's Right to Vote (1920)," National Archives, https://www.archives.gov/milestone-documents/19th-amendment.
22. "Her Life: The Woman behind the New Deal," Frances Perkins Center, https://francesperkinscenter.org/life-new/.
23. Evan K. Rose, "The Rise and Fall of Female Labor Force Participation During World War II in the United States," Cambridge University Press, September 7, 2018, https://www.cambridge.org/core/journals/journal-of-economic-history/article/rise-and-fall-of-female-labor-force-participation-during-world-war-ii-in-the-united-states/66C7D7FD7F6424DF40625E913DDC788F.
24. "The Equal Pay Act of 1963," US Equal Employment Opportunity Commission, https://www.eeoc.gov/statutes/equal-pay-act-1963.
25. "Civil Rights Act (1964)," National Archives, https://www.archives.gov/milestone-documents/civil-rights-act.

26. *Phillips v. Martin Marietta Corporation* (The US Supreme Court, January 25, 1971).
27. Office for Civil Rights, "Title IX of the Education Amendments of 1972," US Department of Health & Human Services, October 20, 2022, https://www.hhs.gov/civil-rights/for-individuals/sex-discrimination/title-ix-education-amendments/index.html.
28. Nicholas Salter, "A Brief History of Female Fortune 500 CEOs," Fisher College of Business, The Ohio State University, March 31, 2021, https://fisher.osu.edu/blogs/leadreadtoday/a-brief-history-female-fortune-500-ceos.
29. "The Pregnancy Discrimination Act of 1978," US Equal Employment Opportunity Commission, https://www.eeoc.gov/statutes/pregnancy-discrimination-act-1978.
30. "Sandra Day O'Connor: First Woman on the Supreme Court," Supreme Court of the United States, https://www.supremecourt.gov/visiting/exhibitions/SOCExhibit/Section3.aspx.
31. "Who Was Sally Ride?," NASA, June 18, 2014, https://www.nasa.gov/audience/forstudents/k-4/stories/nasa-knows/who-was-sally-ride-k4.html.
32. Stuart Taylor Jr., "Sex Harassment on Job Is Illegal," *New York Times*, June 20, 1986, https://www.nytimes.com/1986/06/20/us/sex-harassment-on-job-is-illegal.html.
33. Deborah Sweeney, "How HR 5050 Changed Entrepreneurship for Women," *Forbes*, August 21, 2018, https://www.forbes.com/sites/deborahsweeney/2018/08/21/how-hr-5050-changed-entrepreneurship-for-women/?sh=2dc3f2ab11a5.
34. "Supreme Court Finds Employers Liable for Sexual Harassment for Supervisors, but Creates Affirmative Defense," Findlaw, October 16, 2017, https://corporate.findlaw.com/human-resources/supreme-court-finds-employers-liable-for-sexual-harassment-for.html.
35. "FLSA Protections for Employees to Pump Breast Milk at Work," United States Department of Labor, revised January 2023, https://www.dol.gov/agencies/whd/fact-sheets/73-flsa-break-time-nursing-mothers.
36. Elyse Fitzpatrick and Eric Schumacher, *Worthy: Celebrating the Value of Women* (Minneapolis, MN: Bethany House, 2020).

CHAPTER 3: APPROACHING OUR WORK AS CHRISTIANS

1. Romans 8:28.
2. Eugene H. Peterson, *A Long Obedience in the Same Direction: Discipleship in an Instant Society* (Downers Grove, IL: InterVarsity Press, 1996), 138.
3. David M. Shaw, "The Already and Not-Yet Kingdom," The Gospel Coalition, April 8, 2018, https://au.thegospelcoalition.org/article/already-not-yet-kingdom/.
4. John Mark Comer, *Garden City: Work, Rest, and the Art of Being Human* (Grand Rapids, MI: Zondervan, 2015), 120.
5. Dictionary.com, s.v. "ambassador (*n.*)," https://www.dictionary.com/browse/ambassador.
6. Austin Burkhart, "'Avodah': What It Means to Live a Seamless Life of Work, Worship, and Service," Institute for Faith, Work & Economics, March 31, 2015, https://tifwe.org/avodah-a-life-of-work-worship-and-service/.
7. Ibid.
8. Gustaf Wingren, *Luther on Vocation*, trans. Carl C. Rasmussen (Eugene, OR: Wipf & Stock, 2004), 10.
9. C. S. Lewis, *Mere Christianity* (New York: Simon and Schuster, 1996), 129.
10. Timothy Keller and Katherine Leary Alsdorf, *Every Good Endeavor* (New York: Dutton, 2012), 184.
11. Center for Faith & Work, https://faithandwork.com/about/.
12. Katherine Leary Alsdorf, "A Reformed Theology of Work in New York," essay in *Reformed Public Theology: A Global Vision for Life in the World*, ed. Matthew Kaemingk (Grand Rapids, MI: Baker Academic, 2021), 95.
13. Sebastian Traeger and Greg Gilbert, *The Gospel at Work: How the Gospel Gives New Purpose and Meaning to Our Jobs* (Grand Rapids, MI: Zondervan, 2018).
14. "First Amendment and Religion," United States Courts, https://www.uscourts.gov/educational-resources/educational-activities/first-amendment-and-religion.
15. Traeger and Gilbert, *The Gospel at Work*, 123.

16. Douglas McKelvey, Ned Bustard, and Pete Peterson, *Every Moment Holy* (Nashville: Rabbit Room Press, 2019), 6–7.
17. Steven Garber, *Visions of Vocation: Common Grace for the Common Good* (Downers Grove, IL: IVP Books, 2014).

CHAPTER 4: A SEASON FOR EVERYTHING

1. Nancy Ray, "Calling vs. Assignment," *Work and Play with Nancy Ray* podcast, May 14, 2019, https://podcasts.apple.com/us/podcast/calling-vs-assignment/id1460851854?i=1000438067295.
2. John Piper, *Don't Waste Your Life* (Wheaton, IL: Crossway, 2004), 116.
3. *Merriam-Webster*, s.v. "assignment (*n.*)," https://www.merriam-webster.com/dictionary/assignment.
4. J. D. Greear, "What Does God Require? Not Success, but Faithfulness," J. D. Greear Ministries, September 25, 2014, https://jdgreear.com/what-does-god-require-not-success-but-faithfulness/.
5. Ibid.
6. Steven Garber, *Visions of Vocation: Common Grace for the Common Good* (Downers Grove, IL: IVP Books, 2014), 18, emphasis mine.
7. Timothy Keller and Katherine Leary Alsdorf, *Every Good Endeavor: Connecting Your Work to God's Work* (New York: Dutton, 2012), 52.
8. Frederick Buechner, *Wishful Thinking: A Seeker's ABC* (London: Mowbray, 1994), 118–19.
9. Amy L. Sherman, *Kingdom Calling: Vocational Stewardship for the Common Good* (Downers Grove, IL: IVP Books, 2011), 20.
10. Jeremiah 28:7.
11. Justin Whitmel Earley, *The Common Rule: Habits of Purpose for an Age of Distraction* (Downers Grove, IL: InterVarsity Press, 2019), 16.
12. Garber, *Visions of Vocation*, 239.
13. Amy L. Sherman, *Kingdom Calling: Vocational Stewardship for the Common Good* (Downers Grove, IL: IVP Books, 2011).

CHAPTER 5: DEALING WITH CHALLENGES

1. Timothy Keller, *The Prodigal Prophet: Jonah and the Mystery of God's Mercy* (New York: Viking, 2018), 138.
2. A. W. Tozer, *Man: The Dwelling Place of God* (Chicago: Moody Publishers, 2008), 76.
3. Oliver Burkeman, *Four Thousand Weeks: Time Management of Mortals* (New York: Farrar, Straus and Giroux, 2021), 30.
4. Elisabeth Elliot, *Let Me Be a Woman* (Carol Stream, IL: Tyndale House Publishers, 2004), 17, Kindle.
5. Richard Smith, "What Is the Difference between Envy and Jealousy?," *Psychology Today*, January 3, 2014, https://www.psychologytoday.com/us/blog/joy-and-pain/201401/what-is-the-difference-between-envy-and-jealousy, emphasis mine.
6. Linda Dillow, *Calm My Anxious Heart: A Woman's Guide to Finding Contentment* (Colorado Springs: NavPress, 2020), 5.
7. Hesha Abrams, "How to Keep Calm and Defuse Tensions in Conflict," *How to Be Awesome at Your Job* podcast, December 1, 2022, https://awesomeatyourjob.com/821-how-to-keep-calm-and-defuse-tensions-in-conflict-with-hesha-abrams/?ck_subscriber_id=1169807077.
8. This quote has been attributed to various people, including Robert Heinlein, but it's commonly known as "Hanlon's Razor."
9. Steven Garber, *Visions of Vocation: Common Grace for the Common Good* (Downers Grove, IL: IVP Books, 2014), 185.
10. Revelation 21:5.
11. Jerry Bridges, *Respectable Sins: The Truth about Anger, Jealousy, Worry, and Other Stuff We Accept* (Colorado Springs: NavPress, 2013).

CHAPTER 6: LEADING WITH CONFIDENCE

1. Elisabeth Elliot, *Let Me Be a Woman* (Carol Stream, IL: Tyndale House Publishers, 2004), 43.

2. John Maxwell, "Your Influence Inventory," *The John Maxwell Leadership Podcast*, April 17, 2019, https://johnmaxwellleadershippodcast.com/episodes/john-maxwell-your-influence-inventory.
3. John Mark Comer, *Garden City: Work, Rest, and the Art of Being Human* (Grand Rapids, MI: Zondervan, 2017), 22, emphasis mine.
4. Ashley Gorman, Instagram post, November 13, 2022, @ashmarvgorman.
5. Jessica Bennett, "How to Overcome 'Impostor Syndrome,'" *New York Times*, https://www.nytimes.com/guides/working-womans-handbook/overcome-impostor-syndrome.
6. Katty Kay and Claire Shipman, *The Confidence Code: The Science and Art of Self-Assurance—What Women Should Know* (New York: HarperBusiness, 2018), xviii.
7. "10 Reasons Why the World Needs More Women in Leadership Roles," Natural HR, March 23, 2021, https://www.naturalhr.com/2021/03/23/10-reasons-why-the-world-needs-more-women-in-leadership-roles/.
8. "Women in Leadership," Women Deliver, March 3, 2020, https://womendeliver.org/womensleadership/.
9. Kay and Shipman, *The Confidence Code*, 49.
10. Tom Kolditz, "Why the Military Produces Great Leaders," *Harvard Business Review*, February 6, 2009, https://hbr.org/2009/02/why-the-military-produces-grea.
11. "What Is Servant Leadership?," Greenleaf Center for Servant Leadership, https://www.greenleaf.org/what-is-servant-leadership/.
12. I've heard this idea expressed by my former colleague, Brent Leatherwood, although the original source is unknown.
13. Dorothy L. Sayers, "Why Work?," in *Letters to a Diminished Church: Passionate Arguments for the Relevance of Christian Doctrine* (Nashville: W Publishing Group, 2004), 133, emphasis mine.
14. David T. Harvey, *Rescuing Ambition* (Wheaton, IL: Crossway, 2010), 27.
15. Amy L. Sherman, *Kingdom Calling: Vocational Stewardship for the Common Good* (Downers Grove, IL: IVP Books, 2011), 20.
16. Proverbs 31:20.
17. Sherman, *Kingdom Calling*, 20.

18. Catherine Gates, *The Confidence Cornerstone* (Powell, OH: Author Academy Elite, 2020).
19. Katty Kay and Claire Shipman, *The Confidence Code: The Science and Art of Self-Assurance—What Women Should Know* (New York: HarperBusiness, 2018).
20. Simon Sinek, *Leaders Eat Last: Why Some Teams Pull Together and Others Don't* (New York: Portfolio Penguin, 2014).

CHAPTER 7: NAVIGATING GENDER AND RACIAL DISCRIMINATION

1. Rebecca McLaughlin, *Jesus through the Eyes of Women: How the First Female Disciples Help Us Know and Love the Lord* (Austin, TX: The Gospel Coalition, 2022), 13.
2. Galatians 3:28.
3. Rebecca McLaughlin, "Jesus Changed Everything for Women," The Gospel Coalition, March 22, 2021, https://www.thegospelcoalition.org/article/jesus-changed-everything-women/.
4. Eliezer Segal, "Who Has Not Made Me a Woman," My Jewish Learning, July 5, 2018, https://www.myjewishlearning.com/article/who-has-not-made-me-a-woman/.
5. McLaughlin, *Jesus through the Eyes of Women*, 13.
6. "Gender-Biased Sex Selection," United Nations Population Fund, https://www.unfpa.org/gender-biased-sex-selection.
7. Al Jazeera Staff, "US, Canada Commemorate Missing and Murdered Indigenous Women," Al Jazeera, May 5, 2022, https://www.aljazeera.com/news/2022/5/5/us-canada-commemorate-missing-and-murdered-indigenous-women.
8. "The Nobel Peace Prize 2018," NobelPrize.org, https://www.nobelprize.org/prizes/peace/2018/murad/facts/.
9. "Nobel Lecture Given by Nobel Peace Prize Laureate 2018, Nadia Murad," United Nations, December 11, 2018, https://iraq.un.org/en/170058-nobel-lecture-given-nobel-peace-prize-laureate-2018-nadia-murad.
10. "Race/Color Discrimination," US Equal Employment Opportunity Commission, https://www.eeoc.gov/racecolor-discrimination.

11. "Natural Hair Discrimination FAQ," Legal Defense Fund, February 13, 2023, https://www.naacpldf.org/natural-hair-discrimination/.
12. Chelsea Stein, "MSU Research Exposes Discrimination against Black Women with Natural Hair," Michigan State University, September 18, 2020, https://broad.msu.edu/news/msu-research-exposes-discrimination-against-black-women-with-natural-hair/.
13. "Crown Act Research Studies," https://www.thecrownact.com/research-studies.
14. Rebecca McLaughlin, *Jesus through the Eyes of Women: How the First Female Disciples Help Us Know and Love the Lord* (Austin, TX: The Gospel Coalition, 2022).

CHAPTER 8: THE SECRET TO FLOURISHING

1. Søren Kierkegaard, *Kierkegaard's Journals and Notebooks*, vol. 4, ed. Niels Jørgen Cappelørn et al. (Princeton, NJ: Princeton University Press, 2011), 74.
2. St. Augustine, *Confessions*, trans. Henry Chadwick (Oxford: Oxford World's Classics, 2009), 3.
3. Dane C. Ortlund, *Gentle and Lowly: The Heart of Christ for Sinners and Sufferers* (Wheaton, IL: Crossway, 2021), 20–21.
4. Kelly M. Kapic, *You're Only Human: How Your Limits Reflect God's Design and Why That's Good News* (Grand Rapids, MI: Brazos Press, 2022), 6.
5. Eric W. Hayden, "Charles H. Spurgeon: Did You Know?," https://www.christianitytoday.com/history/issues/issue-29/charles-h-spurgeon-did-you-know.html.
6. C. H. Spurgeon, *Lectures to My Students: A Selection from Addresses Delivered to the Students of the Pastors' College, Metropolitan Tabernacle* (Grand Rapids, MI: Baker Book House, 1977), 260.
7. "Shabbat: What Is Shabbat?," Aleph Beta, https://www.alephbeta.org/shabbat/what-is-the-sabbath.
8. Jen Pollock Michel, *In Good Time: 8 Habits for Reimagining Productivity, Resisting Hurry, and Practicing Peace* (Grand Rapids, MI: Baker Books, 2022), 48.

9. Ibid.
10. Ibid.
11. Walter Brueggemann, *Sabbath as Resistance: Saying No to the Culture of Now* (Louisville, KY: Westminster John Knox Press, 2014), 107.
12. Eugene H. Peterson, "The Pastor's Sabbath," *Christianity Today*, May 19, 2004, https://www.christianitytoday.com/pastors/leadership-books/prayerpersonalgrowth/lclead04-2.html.
13. Dan B. Allender, *Sabbath* (Nashville, TN: Thomas Nelson, 2009), 4–5.
14. Scotty Smith, "Deep Rest," The Gospel Coalition, March 18, 2018, https://www.thegospelcoalition.org/blogs/scotty-smith/deep-rest/.
15. John Mark Comer, *The Ruthless Elimination of Hurry: How to Stay Emotionally Healthy and Spiritually Alive in Our Current Chaos* (Colorado Springs: WaterBrook, 2019).
16. Ruth Haley Barton, *Sacred Rhythms: Arranging Our Lives for Spiritual Transformation* (Downers Grove, IL: IVP Books, 2022).
17. Kelly M. Kapic, *You're Only Human: How Your Limits Reflect God's Design and Why That's Good News* (Grand Rapids, MI: Brazos Press, 2022).

CHAPTER 9: CAN WOMEN HAVE IT ALL?

1. Frances R. Havergal, "Take My Life and Let It Be," hymn, 1874.
2. Jory MacKay, "Time Anxiety: How to Deal with the Feeling That You 'Never Have Enough Time,'" Rescue Time (blog), November 10, 2020, https://blog.rescuetime.com/time-anxiety/.
3. Jen Pollock Michel, *In Good Time: 8 Habits for Reimagining Productivity, Resisting Hurry, and Practicing Peace* (Grand Rapids, MI: Baker Books, 2022), 103.
4. Psalm 90:12.
5. Psalm 1:1–3.
6. Vaneetha Rendall Risner, "What Does It Really Mean to Be #Blessed?," Desiring God, April 28, 2016, https://www.desiringgod.org/articles/what-does-it-really-mean-to-be-blessed.
7. Jordan Raynor, *Redeeming Your Time: 7 Biblical Principles for Being Purposeful, Present, and Wildly Productive* (Colorado Springs: WaterBrook, 2021), 80.

8. Tim Challies, *Do More Better: A Practical Guide to Productivity* (Minneapolis, MN: Cruciform Press, 2015), 16.
9. *Merriam-Webster*, s.v. "habit (*n.*)," https://www.merriam-webster.com/dictionary/habit.
10. Annie Dillard, *The Writing Life* (New York: HarperPerennial, 2013), 32.
11. David Allen, *Getting Things Done: The Art of Stress-Free Productivity* (New York: Penguin Books, 2001), 277.
12. Revelation 22:1.
13. Hebrews 4:3.
14. Revelation 21:3–4.
15. Matt Perman, *What's Best Next: How the Gospel Transforms the Way You Get Things Done* (Grand Rapids, MI: Zondervan, 2014).
16. Tim Challies, *Do More Better: A Practical Guide to Productivity* (Minneapolis, MN: Cruciform Press, 2017).
17. Justin Whitmel Earley, *The Common Rule: Habits of Purpose for an Age of Distraction* (Downers Grove, IL: IVP Books, 2019).

AFTERWORD

1. C. H. Spurgeon, *Morning and Evening* (Grand Rapids, MI: Discovery House, 2016), November 7.
2. Michael Sobolik, "The Girl and the Sea," *Medium*, May 9, 2021, https://michaelsobolik.medium.com/the-girl-and-the-sea-9c40db002bc4.